Richard Blome, Thomas Lynch

A Description of the Island of Jamaica

Richard Blome, Thomas Lynch
A Description of the Island of Jamaica
ISBN/EAN: 9783337330200
Printed in Europe, USA, Canada, Australia, Japan
Cover: Foto ©Andreas Hilbeck / pixelio.de

More available books at **www.hansebooks.com**

A DESCRIPTION,

Of the ISLAND of

JAMAICA;

With the other Isles and Territories in *AMERICA*, to which the *English* are Related, *viz.*

Barbadoes,
St. Christophers,
Nevis, or Mevis,
Antego,
St. Vincent,
Dominica,
Montserrat,
Anguilla,

Barbada,
Bermudes,
Carolina,
Virginia,
Maryland,
New-York,
New England,
New-Found-Land.

Taken from the Notes of Sr. *Thomas Linch* Knight, Governour of *Jamaica*; and other Experienced Persons in the said Places. Illustrated with Maps.

Published by *Richard Blome*.

LONDON,
Printed by T. Milbourn, and sold by the Book-sellers of *London*, and *Westminster*, 1672.

TO HIS
SACRED MAJESTY
CHARLES II.

King of *England*, *Scotland*, *France*, and *Ireland*, &c.

𝔇𝔯𝔢𝔞𝔡 𝔖𝔬𝔳𝔢𝔯𝔞𝔦𝔤𝔫,

HIS small Treatise, or Description, of Your Majesties Dominions and Territories in *America*,

humbly presents its self unto Your Royal Patronage, by the hands of

Your MAJESTIES most

humble and obedient

Subject and Servant,

Richard Blome.

THE PREFACE TO THE READER.

H*Aving the Favour of some* Notes *from my Honoured Friend* Sir Thomas Linch Knight, *about the* Description *of the Island of Jamaica, whose Worth and Ingenuity hath lately merited from his* Majesty *the Government of the said Isle.; as likewise the opportunity of several* Papers

To the Reader.

pers *relating to the* Affairs *and* Description *of the other* Isles *and* Territories *in* America, *wherein the*
English *are concerned, which I received from the hands of several
of my* Friends *who are related
thereunto, I thought them very
fit to be* Published. *The said*
Notes *and* Papers *I have digested
into a clearer and more compen-
dious Method; being brief* De-
scriptions *thereof, which this small*
Treatise *only aimeth at; and not
to trouble the* Reader *with large
and unnecessary discourses no ways
proper for the Design in hand:
for by that means, I might (by the
help of a large* Print *which some*
Publisher *of* Books *call* Ornamen-
tal) *have put them to an unnecessary charge in Buying, and as
great a trouble in Reading. I
have also added some* Maps *for
the*

To the Reader.

the more utility thereof, which were taken from the Latest Sur-*veys.*

Rich. Blome.

Errata.

In Page 126. Line 8. the word [*not*] to be omitted.

A NEW SURVEY,

OR,

Description of the Island of
JAMAICA.

THE Island of *Jamaica* lyeth betwixt the *Tropicks* in the 17. and 18. Degrees of *Northern Latitude*; and beareth from off the Island of *Hispaniola* Eastward, about 35. Leagues. *Its Scituation.*

From the Island of *Cuba* Northwards, about 20. Leagues.

From

Jamaica.

From *Porto Bello* Southwards, about 160. Leagues.

From *Carthagena* South-easterly about 140. Leagues.

From *Rio de la Hache* in the Continent South-easterly, 160. Leagues.

The forme and Extent of the Isle.

Its Form and Extent. It is something inclined to an Oval Forme, being from East to West 170 Miles in length; and from North to South in the midst where it is broadest about 70, it waxing narrower and narrower at both extream ends.

From East to West along the the midst of the *Isle* runns a continued Ridge of lofty *Mountains* which are full of fresh *Springs*, whence flow the many Rivers that

Jamaica.

so plentifully waters the *Island*, to the great refreshment and accommodation of the *Inhabitants*.

The Soyle, Fertility, &c.

It is in most parts (especially the north) of a rich and fat *Soyle*, being of a *blackish Earth*, in many places mixt with a *Clay*, and in some, as the south West *Parts*, it is of a more red and loose *Earth*, but every where incomparable apt to produce, and liberally to answer the *Cultivators* cost and paines for what is planted; being alwayes *Springing*, and its *Trees* and *Plants* never disrobed of their *summer Livery*, every month being to them as our *May*, or *April*.

Here are many *Savanas* which are intermixed with the *Hills* and *Woods*, (especially in the North

Its Soyl, and Fertility.

Savanas, formerly Fields of Indian Maiz.

Jamaica.

North and South parts, where are great store of wild *Cattel*) which by report were sometimes *Feilds* of *Indian Maiz*, or *Wheat*, which when the *Spaniards* became *Masters* of the *Isle*, they converted to *Pasture* for the feeding of their *Cattel*; bringing hither from *Spain*, *Horses*, *Cowes*, *Hoggs*, and *Asenegros* for a Breed, after they had destroyed all the *Natives*, or *Indians*, which according to calculation, did amount to about 60000. which *Cattel* did exceedingly encrease, witness the great heards of *Horses*, and other *Cattel*, that are now wild in the *Woods*; besides the great quantities of *Cows* that have been Killed by the *English*, since they became *Masters* thereof: And these *Savanas* are the most barren, as being so long made use of

Jamaica.

of without Tillage; yet doth they produce such great Plenty of *Grass*, that the *English* are constrained oft-times to burn it up.

The Air, and Temperature.

The *Air* is here more temperate then in any of the *Caribbee Isles*, as seated more Northerly, and of as mild a temperature (as to *Heate*) as any place between the *Tropicks*, being always cooled with fresh Breezes, that constantly bow easterly, and refreshed with frequent *Showers* of *Rain*, and such *Dews* that fall in the night (much quickning the growth of what is *Planted*) that it may truly be called *temperate* and healthful; and by reason of its continuall *Verdure* (as I have before noted) exceeding Delightful.

The Air & Temperature

And

Jamaica.

And it is observed that the west and east *Parts* of the *Isle* are most subject to *Raine* and *Windes*; and the *Woods* being also thick, and close, rendreth the *Aire* less agreeable, then the North and South Parts, which are more plain and open, and less subject to *Raine* and *Winds*. The *Mountaines* which run along the midle of the *Isle* from one extreame point to the other, are much Cooler then the other parts, insomuch that oft times in the mornings there is small white *Frosts*.

Huricanes not in this Isle.

This *Island* is in no parts troubled with those *storms* of *Wind* called *Huricanes*, which all the *Caribbee Isles* are much pestered with, having somtimes by the violence of those *Gusts*, their *Ships* forced out of their *Roads*; and on *Shore*, their *Houses* blown down, and *provisions*,

visions, &c. rooted out of the Earth.

The Weather.

The *Weather* of this *Isle* is less certain then in the rest of the *Caribbee Islands*; the most observable wett *seasons* are in *November* or *May*; there being no seemable *Winter* but by a little more *Rain*, and *Thunder*, in the winter months.

[margin: The Winter known only by Rain and Thunder]

The winds here constantly blow all the day from nine in the morning easterly, and become more fresher as the *Sun* mounteth higher, by reason of which, at midd-day *Travel* or *Labour* is sufferable. But from eight at *Night* to about eight in the *Morning*, it frequently blows Westerly; and with these *Winds*, or *Breezes*, the

Vessells get out of the *Harbours*, and ply to wind-ward.

Dayes, & Nights almost equal. There is scarce any sencible lengthning or shortning of the *Days* or *Nights*, but are almost alwayes of an equal length.

The Sea *ebbs* and *flowes* seldome above a foot.

Hurricanes are here never known, as before I have noted; nor hath any *Vessel* been lost, or cast away on the *Coast*, since the *English* were *Masters* of it.

The Commodities, which this Island Produceth.

This *Isle* hath, and produceth many excellent *Commodities* and that in exceeding great Plenty, as *Sugars* so good, that they out-sell those of the *Barbadoes* 5. s. per Cent. there being at present about 70. *Sugar*

Jamaica.

rks, which may produce   Sugars.
10 thousand weight of
ose still encreasing, and
ers a going up.

the principal, and most   Cocao.
Commodity of the *Isle*,
hall anon take occasion
of more at large; and
reason of the aptness of
d to produce and beare
other places: here being
above 60. *Cocao Walks*,
undance of young *Walks*
e a growing up, and still
anting, so that in time
come the only noted
that *Commodity* in the
hich is so much made use
and other *Nations*, but
iter measure by the *Spa-*
ho alone are enough to
e product of the *Isle*; so
e is no fear that it will
be-

Jamaica.

become a drugg, and lye upon the hands of the *Planter*.

Indico — *Indico* this *Isle* produceth very good, there being at present more then 60. *Indico Works*, which may produce about 50000. weight of *Indico per. Annum*, and do likewise much encrease.

Cotton. — *Cotton* here hath an especial fineness, and is by all preferred before that of the *Carribbee Isles*.

Tobacco: — *Tobacco* is here indifferent good, being estemed better then that of the *Barbadoes*, but it is not much planted, only a sufficiency to serve themselves; the other Commodities being more beneficial.

Hydes — *Hydes*, of which great quantityes have been Yearly made, and are found to be very large and good.

Tortoise Shells. — Great store of *Tortoises* are taken

Jamaica.

ken on this *Coast*, whose meat (being excellent) they eat, and their *Shells* so much esteemed here in *England* for several curious *Works*, finds good vent.

Here are great variety of *Woods* for *Dyers*, as *Fustick*, *Red-Wood*, a kind of *Logg-Wood*, &c. also *Cædar*, *Mothogeney*, *Brasilletto*, *Lignum-Vitæ*, *Ebony*, *Granadilla*, and many other excellent sweet smelling, and curious *Woods* fitt for choise *Works*, whose names are as yet not known; nor indeed their excellencies; but are exported in great quantities. *Curious Woods.*

Copper, they are assured is in this *Isle*, for they have seen the *Ore*, wrought out of a *Mine* here; and by the *Spaniards* report, the *Bells* that hung in the great Church of St. *Iago*, were cast of the Copper of this *Island*. *Copper.*

Silver

Silver. *Silver* may probably be here, as well as in *Cuba*, and in the *Maine*; and the *English* have been shewed where the *Spaniards* had found a *Silver Mine*, behind the *Mountains* west of *Cagway*.

Ambergreece. *Ambergreece* (according to the *Spaniards* report) hath been often found on this *Coast*.

Salt. *Salt*, this *Island* might make great quantities, there being already 3. good and very large *Salt-ponds*, containing neare 4000. *Acres* of ground; but as yet they make no more then for their own use: although there was made in one *Yeare* about 10000 *Bushells*; and the manager thereof, *Cap. Jo. Noye*, did affirm that he could have made as many *Tunns* if they had had Vent.

Saltpeter. *Saltpeter* hath been found in many parts of the *Island*.

Ginger

Jamaica.

Ginger grows better in this *Isle*, then in many of the *Carribbe Islands*; of which here is sufficiency planted. <small>Ginger.</small>

Codd-pepper which is so commonly used in all the *West Indies*, grows plentifully here. <small>Cod-Pepper.</small>

Piemente, or *Jamaica Pepper*, a spice of the form of *East-India Pepper*, very Aromatical, and of a curious *Gousto*, having the mixt taste of divers *Spices*, grows here in great plenty, wild in the *Mountains*. But the *Spaniards* did sett a high esteeme thereon, and exported it as a very choise *Commodity*, as indeed it is; and now it is begun to be planted by the *English*, and will become a good *Commodity*. <small>Piemente.</small>

Drugs are here in great abundance, as *Guacum*, *China-Roots*, *Sasapharilla*, *Cashia Fistula*, *Tamerindes*, <small>Druggs.</small>

Gumms.

merinds, *Vinillos*, *Achiots* or *Anetto*, which is like to prove a good *Commodity*. Here are also divers *Gums*, and *Roots*, wherewith experienced *Planters* do cure many *Hurts*, *Ulcers*, and *Distempers* of the Body. And by the report of an intelligent *Doctor*, which made it his business to search after such things, here are likewise *Contrayerna*, *Cyperas*, *Aloes*, *Assole Pie*, *Adjuntum*, *Nigrum*, *Cucumis*, *Agrestis*, *Sumach*, *Acacia*, *Miselto*, with many other *Druggs*, *Balsoms* and *Gums*, whose *names* are not known, or remembred: but the *Planters* begin to be more expert in these *Drugs*, and endeavour to encrease them, and supply *England* therewith.

Cochaneil.

Cochaneil is produced by a *Plant* that grows in this *Isle*, but as

Jamaica.

as yet the *English* want experience to husband it; easterly *Winds*, and many other things being Enemies to its growth, besides the difficulty of makeing it.

These with some others are the Commodities that this *Island* produceth, which if well improved, would soon become the best, and Richest *Plantation* that ever the *English* were, (or are like to be) Masters of.

I shall in the next place give you an Account of the management of a *Cocao Walk*, with a calculation of its *Costs*, and *Profits*, as it was lately estimated by that judicious and great encourager of the Planters, *S. Tho. Modiford Baronett*, late *Governour* of the said *Island*.

Directions

Jamaica.

Directions about a Cocao Walk.

	l.	*s.*
First, take up 5 or 600. *Acres* of *Land,* which be sure choose in a good place proper to produce the *Cocao,* which will cost for the *Surveying* and *Patent*	010	0
For 3 *Negro men,* and as many *Negro women* at 20 *l.* per head	120	0
For 4 *White Servants,* with their Passage and Dyet for a year	080	0
For 20 *Axes,* 20 *Bills,* and 20 *Hoos* for them	005	0

For

Jamaica.

For 6. *Negroes Dyet*, for Six months at 2 *s.* *per Day*, until you have some provisions *Grown* in your *Plantation*. } *l.* *s.* 018 5

For an *Overseer* to look after the *Servants*, for his *Wages* and *Diet* at 40 *s. per Month* } *l.* *s.* 024 0

In all 257 5

And for the employing these *Servants* in your *Plantation* as followeth: supposing them to *Land*, and to be on the *Plantation* the first of *March*, and that they have by the middle of that month (as they may very easily) cleared a convenient place, and built fitting houseing for the lodging

ing them. Then put them to falling, cleaning, and planting a *Potato peece* of 4. *Acres*, which *ten hands* will very well do by the middle of *April*: after this, you may clean, and plant with *Rue* and *Plantin-Trees*, until the last of *February*, which is above 10 *Months*; in which time they may with ease have cleansed and Planted 21. *Acres*, besides keeping them clean which are Planted, and are still a Planting; and in this time, which compleats the *Year*, you may be full of *Potatoes* and *Corn*, and within 2. *Months* of the new *Year*, with *Plantins*, and a small stock of *Hoggs*, and *Fowles*; so that you will be at no more charge for *Provisions* for your *Servants*. And then to keep this clean, and to plant the *Cocao-Walks*; and for five more *Negro Men*,

Jamaica.

Men, and 5. *Negro-Women* to buy about the first of *March* following, at 20 *l. per Negroe* comes to 200 *l.*

And in that *Month* you will have Planted *Cocao-Trees* out of the *Nuts*, or *Seed*, betwixt all the *Rows* of the *Plantin-Trees*, that are 6. *Foot* high; so that by the first of *June*, the whole 21 *Acres* that were planted the last *Year*, will be full of *Cocao-Trees*, and by that time you will have (besides much other work done) 21. *Acres* of *Cocao-Trees* in the ground; which in less then 4. years, from the Planting, will begin to bear *Cods*, and in a year after, produce compleat Cropps. And according to experience, an *Acre* doth produce every year about 1000. pound *Weight*; which at *Jamaica* is worth 4*l. per Cent.* which for the 21 *Acres*, doth

doth amount unto 840 *l. per Ann.* *Although* this last year, by reason their *Cropps* were blasted, it is at present far dearer, the *Hundred weight* at *London* being now worth 18. pound *Sterling.*

The charges of gathering and houseing the *Cocao,* is inconsiderable, only *Cloths* or *Baggs* to put it in, which with some other incident charges, may be reckoned at the most (as all things else have been) to Amount to 42. l. 15. s. more, which makes up just 500. l.

Note, that all this that is *Planted,* is done in 15. *months,* and the *Cocao* bears not compleatly until the sixth year from the first begining, or comming; so that you will have four years and nine months at liberty with your *Servants,* either to encrease the *Cocao Walk,* building of convenient

Jamaica.

ent houses, and makeing of *Gardens* for pleasure; or else you may fall on *Ginger*, *Indico*, or some other *Commodity* for present profit, which perhapps may be necessary for such as cannot forbear their Money, until the *Cocoa Walk* doth come to perfection as aforesaid: after which, you will find sufficient profit as is exprest, Sickness, Mortality, and running away Excepted. Yet it cannot be expected, but that as the *Island* encreaseth in this *Commodity*, they must some-what abate the present Price, and content themselves with a more moderate Gaines.

And according to this *Calculation* proportionably a greater or lesser *Cocoa-Walk* may be undertaken, and performed.

Of Servants.

Their Cattle.

In this *Isle* are greater abundance

dance of *Cattle* then in most of the *English Plantations* in *America*; as *Horses*, which are here so plentiful, that a good *Horse* may be bought for 6 or 7 *l*.

Horses.

Their *Cowes* are very large, and so numerous, that although there hath been every Year so many Killed, yet their number seemeth not much to be lessoned.

Cowes.

Assnegroes and *Mules* (both wild and Tame) are very many, which are found to be very serviceable to the *Inhabitants*.

Asnegroes. Mules.

Their *Sheep* are large, and tall, and their *Flesh* good, but their *Wool* is long, hairy, and little worth.

Sheep:

Goats are many, which thrive exceedingly well, the Countrey being very fit for them.

Goats.

Hoggs are here in exceeding great plenty, as well those wild in the *Mountains*, as tame in the

Hoggs.

Plan-

Jamaica.

Plantations, whose *Flesh* is far better tasted, and more nourishing and easier to be digested then those of *England*; which is the reason that it is so much eaten in this *Island*; as indeed throughout the *West-Indies*.

Their Fish.

This *Island* hath both in the *Rivers*, *Bayes*, *Roads*, and *Creeks*, very excellent *Fish*, and in such abundance that it contributes much to the feeding of the *Inhabitants*; and those that frequent this *Isle*, say, that they have few or none of those sorts common to us in *England*; but such great Variety of those appropriated to the *Indies*, that it would be too tedious to Repeat the names of them, if they were known or Remembred.

Excellent Fish in great plenty.

C 4 The

Jamaica.

Tortoise. The principal sort is the *Tortoise*, which they take plentifully on the *Coast*; and about 20. or 30. *Leagues to the Leeward* of port *Negril*, by the Isles of *Camavos*, in the months of *May*, *June*, and *July*, do resort great store of *Ships* from the *Carribbee Isles* to *Victual* and *Load* with this *Fish*, it being reputed to be the wholsomest and best provision in all the *Indies*.

Their Fowls.

great variety of Tame & Wild Fowl. Here are very great plenty of tame *Hens*, *Turkies*, and some *Ducks*; but of wild *Fowle* infinite store, as *Ducks*, *Teale*, *Wigen*, *Geese*, *Turkeys*, *Pigeons*, *Guine-Hens*, *Plovers*, *Flemingo's*, *Snipes*, *Parats*, *Parachetos*, with very many others, whose names are not known.

Jamaica.

The Fruits.

There are great plenty of choise and excellent *Fruits* in this *Island*, as *Oranges, Pome-granates, Cocar-Nuts, Limes, Guavars, Mammes, Alumee-Supotas, Suppotillias, Avocatas, Cashues, Prickle-Aples, Prickle-Pears, Grapes, Sower-Sops, Custard-Aples, Dildowes*, and many others whose names are not known, or too tedious to name, besides *Plantains, Pines*, &c.

Excellent Fruits.

Their Herbes, and Roots.

Here likewise grows very well, all manner of Summer-*Garden-Herbs* and *Roots* common to us in *England*, as *Radish, Lettis, Purseley, Cucumbers, Melons, Parsley, Pot-herbs*, also *Beanes, Pease,*

Herbs & Roots.

Ca-

Jamaica.

Cabbages, Colly-Flowers, &c.

Their Diseases.

Jamaica very healthful.

It hath been experimentally found, that there is no such Antipathy betwixt the constitutions of the *English,* and this clime, for the occasioning Sickness to be Mortal or Contageous, more than in other parts; for if a good *Dyet,* and moderate Exercises are used, without excess of *Drinking,* they may enjoy a competent measure of Health.

Diseases strangers are most subject unto.

The *Diseases* that Strangers are most incident to, are *Dropsies* (occasioned often by ill *diet, drunkeness,* and *slothfulness*) *Calentures* too frequently the product of *Surfits,* also *Feavers,* and *Agues,* which although very troublesome, yet are seldome Mortal.

And

Jamaica.

And the reason of the great Mortality of the *Army*, at their first arrival, was their want of *Provisions*, together with an unwillingness to labour or excercise, joyned with discontent.

Hurtful things.

There are upon this *Island*, very few obnoctious *Beasts*, *Insects*, or *Plants*.

Here is the *Manchonele*, which is a kind of a *Crab*, so common in all the *Caribbee Isles*. — Manchonele.

Here are *Snakes*, and *Guianas*, but no poysonous quality is observed in them. — Snakes, Guianas.

In many of the *Rivers*, and *Land-Ponds*, are *Alligators*, which are very voracious Creatures, yet seldome do they prey upon a Man, as being very easy to be avoided, — Alligators.

for

for he can only move forwards, and that he doth with great Swiftness and Strength, and is as slow in turning. Some are 10, 15, or 20 foot long, their backs are scaly and impenetrable, so that they are hardly to be killed, except in the *Belly* or *Eye*. They have four *Feet* or *Finns* with which they go or swim. They are observed to make no kind of Noise: and the usual course for the getting their Prey, is to lie on the *banks* of *Rivers*, and as any *Beast* or *Fowle* cometh to *drink*, they suddenly seize on them; and the rather, for that they do so much resemble a long peece of dry wood, or some dead thing. And as these *Allegators* are thus obnoctious on the one hand, so are they found to be useful on the other, for their Fat is a Sovereign *Oyntment* for any internal Ach

Jamaica.

Ach or Pain in the *Joynts*, or *Bones*. They have in them *Musk-codds*, which are stronger scented then those of the *East-Indies*, and by this their strong smell, they are discovered, and avoyded; which 'tis supposed the Cattle by instinct of Nature, are also sencible of, and do by that means often shun them. They lay *Eggs* in the Sand by the water-side, which are no bigger than a *Turkeys*, which they cover, and by the heat of the *Sun*, the young ones are hatched, who naturally creep into the water.

Here are also *Muskettoes* and *Merry-wings*, a sort of stinging *Flies* that are troublesome in some parts of the *Isle*, but are seldome found in the *English Plantations*.

Muskettoes. Merry-wings.

Their

Jamaica.

Their Harbours, Roads, and Bays.

This *Island* abounds with good *Bayes*, *Roads*, and *Harbours*: the Principal amongst which are

Port-Royal, formerly called *Cagway*, situate on the extream end of that long point of *Land* which makes the *Harbour*, which is exceeding commodious for *Shipping*, and secured by one of the strongest and most considerable *Castles* that his *Majesty* hath in all *America*, in which are mounted about 60 peeces of *Ordnance*, and is well guarded with *Souldiers*. It is land-lock't by a point of *Land* that runs 12 miles *South-East* from the main of the *Island*, having the great *River* that runs by *Los Angelos*. and St. *Jago* falling into it, where *Ships* do commonly *water*, and conveniently

[margin: Port-Royal.]

Jamaica.

ently *wood*. The *Harbour* is 2. or 3. leagues cross in most places, and hath every where good *Anchorage*, which is so deep, that a *Ship* of a 1000 *Tunn* may lay her sides to the shore of the *Point*, and load, and unload with *planks* a Float: which commodiousness, doth make it to be the most frequented by *Men* of *War*, and *Merchants Ships* of any in the *Island*, and as much Inhabited by the *Merchants, Storehouse-keepers, Vintners, & Alehouse-keepers*, being the only noted place of *Trade* in the *Isle*, and doth contain (since the *English* became *Masters* of it) about 800 *Houses*, being about 12 miles and a half in length, and the houses are as dear-rented as if they stood in well-traded *Streets* in *London*; yet it's situation is very unpleasant and uncommodious, having neither *Earth, Wood*, or *Fresh-water*,

water, but only made up of a hot loose *Sand*, and being thus populous, and so much frequented, as well by *Strangers*, as by the *Planters*, in the negotiation of their Affairs as being the scale of *Trade*, *provisions* are very dear. This *Town* or *Port* is seated about 12 *miles* from the *Metrapolitan Town* of the *Island* called St. *Jago*, or St. *Jago de la vega*, or the *Spanish* Town; of which I shall treat anon.

Port-Morant. — *Port-Morant* in the *Eastern* Point, a very Capacious and secure *Harbour*, where *Ships* do conveniently *Wood*, *Water*, and *Ride* safe from the *Windes*, and about this place is a potent *Colony* of the *English seated*.

Old Harbour. — *Old-Harbour* Westwards, from St. *Jago*, a good *Bay* for *Ships* to *Ride* in.

Point-Negrill. — *Point-Negril* in the extream *Western*

Jamaica.

Western Point, very good and sufficiently convenient, and secure to windward, in which men of *war* do often ply, when they look for the *Spanish Ships*, whence a little *North-west*, was seated the Old town of *Melilla*, founded by *Columbus*, after the shipwrack there; which was the 1st place that the *Spaniards* setled at, and afterwards deserted.

Port-Antonio seated on the *North*, a very safe land-lock't Harbour, only the coming in is somewhat difficult, the Channel being narrowed by a little *Island* that lies off the mouth of the *Port*, being wholly taken up by the Right Honourable, *Charles* Earl of *Carlisle*, Visc. *Howard* of *Morpeth*, Lord *Dacres* of *Gilsland*, Lord Lieutenant of the Counties of *Cumberland* and *Westmerland*, and one of the Lords of his Majesties most Honourable Privy Council, &c.

Port-Antonio.

D Here

Jamaica.

Here are several other good *Bayes*, and *Harbours*, along the *Coast* of this *Island*; the names of which are set down in the *Map*, amongst which, these are very commodious and good, *viz.*

In the *South*-part

Michaels Hole.
Micary Bay.
Allegator Pont.
Point Pedro.
Pallate Bay.
Lewana Bay.
Blewfelds Bay.
Cabaritaes Bay.

} All *very good* and *Commodious Bayes* for Ships.

In the *North*-part

Porto-Maria
Ora Cabessa
Cold-Harbour
Rio-Nova
Montega-Bay
Orang-Bay

} All *very good Bays* for Shipping.

The

Jamaica.

The Towns.

There are at present but three Towns of considerable Note in the Island, to wit,

St. Jago, or *St. Jago de-lavega* *St. Jago.*
seated 6 *Miles* within the Land North-West, in a *Plaine*, by a River, and about 12. miles from *Port-Royal* already treated of, which makes another of the 3 Towns. This town of St. *Jago* when the *Spaniards* were Masters of the *Isle*, was a large *City*, and of great Account, containing about 2600 *Houses*, and for Divine Worship, had 2 *Churches*, 2 *Chappels*, and an *Abbey*; which when the *English* first took the *Isle* (under the conduct of *General Venables*) were destroyed to about 4 or 500 *Houses*, and its *Churches* and *Chap-*
D 2 *pels*

pels to a fewer number, & those that remained were sufficiently Spoiled and haraced. But since the *English* have made a settlement, this *Towne* is now of considerable account; where the *Governour* resideth, and where the chief *Courts* of *Judicature* are held, which makes it to be well resorted unto, and Inhabited; so that most of its ruinous *Houses* are in a faire way of being repaired, and in hopes to arrive to a greater largeness then formerly it was, here being several fair and well built *Houses*: and the *Inhabitants* live in great Pleasure, where they have their *Havana*, in which the better sort recreate themselves every evening in their *Coaches*, or an horse-back, as the Gentry do here in *Hide Park*.

Passage seated on the mouth of the River, six miles distant from

Jamaica.

St. *Jago*, and as many from *Port-Royal*, where there are about 20 *Houses*, built for the conveniency of going to *Port-Royal*; and here is a *Fort* raised by the *English*, the better to secure the same.

In the time of the *Spaniards*, here were several other *Townes* which are now of no Account; of which said *Townes*, these three following were of most note, viz.

Sevilla seated on the North part of the *Island*, once beautified with a *Collegiate-Church*, whose chief bore the title of *Abbot*: amongst whom was *Peter Martyr*, who described the *History* of the *West-Indies* by *Decates*. — *Sevilla*.

Mellila seated in the North East, where *Columbus* mended his Ships at his return from *Veragua*, where he was neer *Ship-wrackt*. — *Mellila*.

Orista

Orista. *Orista* reguards the *South-Sea*, in which are many *Rocks*, and amongst their Banks, some *Isles*, as *Servavilla*, *Quitosvena*, and *Serrana*, where *Augustin Pedro Serrana* lost his *Vessel*, and saved onely himself, and here in a solitary and lone Condition passed away 3 Yeares; at the end of which time he had the company of a *Marriner* for 4 Years more, that was likewise there *Ship-wrackt*, and also alone saved himself.

14 Precincts or Parishes in the Isle. And although there are for the present no more *Townes*, yet the *Island* is divided into 14 *Precincts*, *Divisions*, or *Parishes*; which are set forth in the *Map*; many of which said *Precincts* are well *Inhabited* by the *English*, where they have very good *Plantations*, especially all the southern part from
Point-

Jamaica.

Point-Morant in the East, almost to *Point-Negrillo* in the West, so far as the ridge or chain of *Mountaines* that runneth in the midst of the *Isle*; nor are its northerns *Parts*, (especially near unto the Sea) without *Inhabitants* and *Plantations*, though not so thick as South-wardly about St. *Jago*, but of late have much encreased. And for the better Satisfying the *Reader*, the *Parts* throughout the *Island* where the *English* have made their *Settlements*, are Marked and distinguished in the *Map* by *Cyphers*. See the Mapp.

I cannot certainely affirm the number of the *English* in this *Isle*, but according to the last survey taken and returned into *England* some *Yeares* since, by Sr. *Thomas Modiford*, late *Governour*, each *Precinct*, or *Parish* contained as followeth:

Jamaica.

A general Account of the Precincts, or Parishes, Families, and Inhabitants in Jamaica, taken by order of Sir Thomas Modiford, then Governour as aforesaid.

The Names of the Precincts or Parishes in the Isle.

Parishes.	Families.	Inhabitants.
Port-Royal	500	3500
St. Katherines	658	6270
St. Johns	083	996
St. Andrews	194	1552
St. Davids	080	960
St. Thomas	059	590
Clarindon	143	1430
	1714	15298

Note, that the Four Parishes on the *North*-side of the *Isle*, to witt, St. *George's*, St. *Maries*, St. *Annes*, and St. *James*, as also the *Leeward* most Parish called St. *Elizabeth*

Jamaica.

zabeth, together with these two not named, both adjoyning on St. *Elizabeths*; the one *Eastwards*, and the other *Northwards*, was not as then so particularly surveyed, by reason of their distance, and new *Settlements*, nevertheless they were found according to Calculation, to amount to about 2000 *Inhabitants*. But all these *parts*, as also those seven aforenamed are now exceedingly encreased, being supposed to be encreased to double, if not treble the number. And the great encouragement of gaining Riches, with a pleasant life, doth invite every year abundance of *People* to Inhabite here, quitting their concerns at *Barbadoes*, and other our *American Plantations*; so that in a short time without doubt it will become the most potent and richest *Plantation* in the *West-Indies*.

And

Jamaica.

And besides the aforesaid number of *Inhabitants* in the said 14 *Precincts* or *Parishes*, there are reckoned to belong to the *Island*, of *Privateers, Hunters, Sloop* and *Boatmen* (which ply about the *Isle*) at the least 3000 lusty and stout *Fighting Men*, whose courage hath been sufficiently evidenced in their late exploit, and attempt made against the *Spaniards* at *Panama*.

Their Lawes

Their Lawes. Their *Lawes* are assimulated (as near as may be) to those of *England*, having their several *Courts, Magistrates*, and *Officers*, for the executing of Justice on criminal Offenders, and the hearing and determination of Causes or Controversies betwixt party, and party.

Having thus made a short description

Jamaica. 43

scription of the *Island*, as to its *Scituation*, *Fertility*, *Commodities*, *Harbours*, *Towns*, and *Precincts*, with an estimate of the number of its *Inhabitants*: In the next place, I shall give you the state of the *Isle*, when the *Spaniards* were possessors thereof; and wind up my discourse with some seasonable considerations relating to the *English* Affairs in *America*, with reasons to justifie the first design in taking it, and why his *Majesty* should keep and support it. And of these in order.

The state of the *Spaniards* in this *Island*.

The *Spaniards* first setled on the *North-west* part of the *Isle*, under the Conduct of *Columbus*, and built the Town of *Mellila*, but disliking the

The Spaniards First settlement.

the Scituation, removed to *Oriſtana*; and finding that alſo to be ill ſeated, and unhealthful, again removed, and ſetled at St. *Jago*, or St. *Jago de la vega*, where, with the aſſiſtance of the *Indians*, they built a fair *Town* or *City*, which I have already treated of. And in this *Town* Inhabited all the *Spaniards* that were in the *Iſle* at the Landing of the *Engliſh*, keeping their ſlaves at their ſeveral ſmall *Plantations*, or *Stanchas*, who failed not to bring them ſtore of *Fruits & Proviſions*, which they luxuriouſly ſpent in their houſes, never intending any thing but to live at eaſe and plenty: For on this large and fertile *Iſland*, there was no *Manufacture* or *Commodity* made, except a little *Sugar*, *Tobacco*, and *Cocao*, and thoſe few *Ships* that came hither, traded generally for *Hydes*, *Tallow*,

The Spaniards inclined to Idleneſs.

Jamaica.

Tallow, *Jamaica Pepper*, and *Cocao*, but not to any confiderable account. And the number of Inhabitants did not exceed 3000, of which, half (if not more) were *Slaves*. And the reafon why it was fo thinly peopled, was, becaufe the *Spaniards* generally defire to be in *Nova Hifpana*, or *Hifpaniola*; but chiefly, becaufe this *Ifle* was held in proprieterfhip, by the heirs of the Duke of *Veragua-Columbus*, who received the Revenues, and placed *Governours*, as abfolute Lord of it. And at the firft, it was planted by a kind of *Portugals*, the fociety of whom, the *Spaniards* abhors.

Upon the approach of the *Englifh-Army* after their landing, the *Inhabitants* of St. *Jago* deferted the *Town*, and betook themfelves to the *Mountains*, pretending a Treaty

Treaty with the *English*, untill such time as they had secured their *Women* and *Goods*, and then did they make several attempts, and upon surprisals, murthered many of the *English*; but the *Spaniards* soon growing weary of that wild and mountainous course of Life, perceiving small hopes of expelling the *English*, divers of the *Grandees* got into *Cuba*, who by the *Vice-Roy* of *Mexico*'s order, were commanded back, with a promise of a speedy and considerable supply of men; upon which they returned, somwhat encouraged, and dispersed themselves by *Families*, that they might the better get *provisions*, and avoid the being discovered by the *English*; but this necessitous and unusual course of life, killed many of them, and discouraged the rest; for that in all this time there

Jamaica.

there came to their succour, but 500 *Souldiers*, and those refused to joyn with them, as being so few and sickly; so that they marched back to the *North* of the *Island*, and at a place called St. *Chereras*, did fortify themselves, every day expecting a new body of Men to joyn with them: But the *English* discovering their *quarters*, marched against them. Some few months after, about 30 small *Companies* of the *Spanish Forces* arrives, and immediately very strongly Fortify *Rio Nova*, having *Ordnance*, and great store of *Ammunition*, yet were they speedily and succesfully defeated by the Valour of the *English* under the Conduct of Leiutenant General *Edw. D'oyley*. And this grand disaster, with many petty ill successes caused the *Spaniards* to dispair of regaining the *Island*, and

and to ship off most of their *Plate* and *Women*; and the *Negroes* finding the greatest part of their Masters to be dead, killed the *Governour*, and declined all obedience to the *Spaniards*, appointing a *Black* for their *Governour*. And such was the necessity of the *Spaniards*, that instead of giving them fitting correction, they were constrained to Court them for their assistance; but all their policy would not prevail upon them, for soon after did they submitt to the *English Goverment*, and made discoveries of the *Spaniards* and *Negroes* that would not come in with them, and did further assist the *English* in the taking of them, in which they have been exceeding succesful.

In the year following, the *Spaniards* quite deserted the *Island*, except it were about 30 or 40 of their

Jamaica.

their *Slaves*, who betook themselves to the *Mountaines*, but being afraid of a Discovery, and to be pursued to Death for some *Murthers* they had committed, built themselves *Conoas*, and in them fled to *Cuba*, and never since hath any considerable attempt been made upon them.

The *English* being thus become Masters of the *Island*, formed themselves into a Body, or Colony: Then did they they begin to settle themselves in *Plantations*, whilst others betook themselves to the Sea as *Freebooters* or *Privateers*, the better to secure themselves against the *Spaniards*, and force them to a peace by their frequent annoying them, in seizing such their ships which they could meet with, which proved very succesful unto them. And this caused

caused the *Isle* to be much talked of, and had in esteem by the *English*, who sent them supplies of Men, Provisions, and necessaryes. And thus by little and little it became to be so potent as now it is.

Governours since the English were Masters of the Island.

This Island (since the Englsh have been Masters of it) hath had four Governours.

The first, Leiutenant General *Edward D'oyley*, who before his *Majesties* happy Restauration, was Commander in cheif of all the *English Army* by *Land* and *Sea* in *America*.

The second, the Right Honourable *Thomas* Lord *Winsor*, who is now Lord Leiutenant of the County of *Worcester*. The

Jamaica.

The third, Sr. *Thomas Modyford* Baronet.

And the fourth, and present, Sr. *Thomas Lynch* Knight.

Some Considerations relating to the English Affaires in America, with Reasons to justify the first designe into the Indies.

1. The *Spaniards* would never contract a Peace with the *English* in *America*. 1. Consideration.

2. They have alwayes taken our *Merchants Ships* sayling on these *Coasts*, or forced them into their *Harbours* by distress of *Weather*. 2 Consid.

3. In the Reign of our late *King* (when we had Peace with them throughout *Europe*) they Sacked St. *Christophers, Mevis, Providence,* Sta. *Cruz,* and *Tortugas,* murthering 3 Consid.

ing and carrying away most of the *Inhabitants* into slavery; for which they never made any repairation.

4 Consid. 4. The *Indians*, who are the natural proprietors of *America*, do abominate and hate the *Spaniards* for their cruelty and avarice; and upon every occasion will shew their willingness to give themselves and their Countreys, freely into the power and protection of the *English*.

5 Consid. 5. The pretented first discovery cannot give them a legal power over the genuine right of the *Natives*, nor were they the first discoverers of all those Countreys that they pretend unto.

6 Consid. 6. The *Popes Donation* is of little validity, for he hath given them the Crown of *England*, which of the two he might more legally do, then the *Indies*; for that the *English*

Jamaica.

glish have been subject to his power, the *Indians* never.

7. Possession is not of force to create (though it confirms) a Right, nor can it so alter the property, as to make usurpation (for some time to continue) as a legal, and just pretence of *Dominion*.

8. It is against the fundamental *Lawes* of *Spain* to make a peace, and allow of a *Trade* into the *Indies*; now there being no *medium*, *War* must needs be justifyable where a Peace is not allowable.

9. Their barbarous cruelty in compelling our *Merchants*, and others which they have took *prisoners*, to turn their *Religion*, and to work at their *Forts* and *Mines* at *Mexico*, and elsewhere, from whence they can never return, murthering divers, when upon a *Treaty*, and after promise of fair

7 Consid.

8 Consid.

9 Consid.

E 3

fair quarter, and not Exchanging or Ransoming any, although the *English* have freely given them some *hundreds* of *Prisoners*, doth sufficiently justify any attempt or mischief we can do against them, either in seizing on their *Ships*, or the landing on their Countreys, and the sacking, burning, or taking their *Towns* and *Countreys*, and the dispossessing them thereof.

Some Considerations why his Majesty should keep, preserve, and support this Island.

1 Consid.   1. *Jamaica* is large, and capacious, whose extent I have already noted; so that it is capable of receiving very great numbers of *People*.

2 Consid.   2. It is seated in the heart of the

Jamaica.

the *Spaniards American Territories*; so that the *Spanish Shipps* coming into the *West-Indies*, and sayling from *Port* to *Port*, either make this *Isle*, or may be immediately met by the *Ships* which ply on this *Coast*, which renders it to be of great importance to Us, as well as to the *Spaniards:* for all the *Plate Fleet* which comes from *Carthagena*, steer directly from St. *Domingo* in *Hispaniola*, and from thence must pass by one of the Ends of this *Isle* to recover *Havana*, which is the common Rendevouze of the *Armado*, before it returns home through the *Gulph* of *Florida*. Nor is there any other way whereby to miss this *Isle*, because they cannot in a reasonable time turn it up to the windward of *Hispaniola*, which, though with great difficulty, it might be done, yet

E 4 by

by this means they would loose the security of the said united *Fleet*, which meet at *Havana*, from all parts of the Bay of *Mexico*, *Nombre de dios*, and elsewhere, and so accompany each other home.

3 Consid.   3. *Jamaica* is found to precede all the *English Plantations* in *America*, in the very *Commodities* that are proper to their several *Colonies*, and produceth also of its own *Cocao*, *Hydes*, *Tortoise-shells*, *Wood* for *Dyers*, *Gums*, *Druggs*, and other *Commodities* already treated of; and for *Fruits*, *Fowl*, and *Fish*, infinite store, many of which are unknown unto them. Likewise, such abundance of *Horses*, and *Cowes*, that none other of the *English Plantations* can equalize them.

Commodities Imported, and its Trade   And as this *Island* is found thus advantageous in the furnishing us with such good *Commodities*, so

is

Jamaica.

is it no less profitable in the taking off our *Manufactures*, and *Commodities*, as well of the product of this *Kingdom*, as those from *Forreign parts*. That is to say, all sorts of *Stuffs*, *Fabricks* of *Silks*, *Linnen* both fine and course, *Hatts*, *Gloves*, *Thread*, *Tape*, *Pinns*, *Needles*, *Stockings*, *Shoos*; all sorts of *Apparel*; *Wine*, *Brandy*, *Strong-Beer*; All sorts of *Utensils* of *Iron*, and other *Mettals* for *Carpenters*, *Joyners*, *Smiths*, *Coopers*, *Mill-Wrights*, and other the like *Tradesmen*, that are found useful for the *Planters* service, Also, *Iron*, *Brass*, *Copper*, *Steel*, *Lead* and *Tinn* unwrought; All sorts of *Armes* and *Ammunition*: Also, Servants, and *Negro-Slaves*: And in a word, all *Commodities* that are necessary, and usefull either for the *Back* or *Belly*, are here

Ven-

Vendible. And is observed, that the better the *Commodities* are (especially *Apparrel* and *Ornaments* for the Back) the sooner and better are they Vended.

4 Consid. 4. It appears to be a place of no small concernment, for it hath not only subsisted at the beginning, but bettered its condition, being setled by an Army (the worst kind of people to plant) that have had such grand discouragements from *England*, as want of *pay, provisions*, and *recruits* of *Men*; yet amongst themselves talked of all encouragements to *Plant*, the establishment of *Justice* and *Government*, besides, the frequent attempts of the *Spanish Forces*; and if it thus thrived under these, and such like considerable obstructions, it is more then propable, it will in a short time become a great and profitable Colony

both

Jamaica.

both to the *King* and *Kingdome*; for when well planted, it may bring into his Majesty some *hundred thousand pownds per Annum*. *Barbadoes* (which is so little compared to this) yeilding about 10000*l. per Annum*, and employing about 150 or 200 Sayl of *Ships* yearly.

5. This *Island* being so large and so fertile, it is capable of the receiving those great numbers of people, that are forced to desert the *Caribbee Isles*: Their *Plantations* being worn out, and their *Woods* wasted; as likewise those multitudes of *Vagrants* and *Beggars* that are so great a charge and shame to the Kingdom, if Transported thither, (would by their labours) live both honestly, and plentifully; here being observed to be no beggars, nor such loose *Vagabond people*.

6. This *Island* being well setled,

5 Consid.

6 Consid.

will

will be capable of it self to carry on a *War* against the *Spaniards* in the *West-Indies* (as occasion requireth) because of the conveniences of its *Ports*, and its strength of *Inhabitants* and *Shipping*, having already about 20 or 30 *Sayl* of *Privateers*; and will in a short time be so numerous and potent, that they will become so obnoxious to the *Spaniards*, that probably they will rather admit of a *Trade* into his *Ports* (which would prove a grand advantage both to them, and this Kingdom) than suffer so disadvantageous a *War*. And having thus forced a *Trade*, would gain the acquaintance of the *Natives*, and learn their *Customes*, and method of *Trade*, being much inclined to love the *English* rather than the *Spaniards*.

7. Confid.   7. *Jamaica* seems to be approved

Jamaica. 61

ved above any of the other *Plantations*, in regard so many from all the *English Collonyes* have Transported themselves and their *Estates* to it, who like it so well, that they have no cause or desire to remove.

8. There is now a considerable progress made in the setling of this *Isle*, there being upon it many *Plantations* of *Cocao*, *Sugar*, *Indico*, *Cotton*, and *Provisions*; and Inhabited with many thousand of of people. The *Planters* (for the generality) now living in great delight, and enjoy all things necessary for *Food* and *Rayment* in a liberal measure; and were it well Inhabited, it would very much consume the *English Manufactures*, and encourage *Navigation* and *Merchandize*.

9. It cannot be imputed a disadvantage, that *Jamaica* lyeth so far

8 Consid.

9 Consid.

far off, for thereby are more *Ships* employed; and by consequence, more *Saylors, Shipwrights, Ropemakers*, and many other *Tradesmen* maintained, whose dependance is thereon. Furthermore, if it lay not so far, we could not expect such *Commodities* as it produceth, being appropriate to the *Clyme*; neither is it a small advantage to have such *Commodities* within his *Majesties Dominions* (though at a distance) that are both valued and needed by his *Subjects* and *Neighbours*, especially the *Cocao*.

10. Consideration.

10. And lastly, to conclude, The *English* have one more considerable advantage by this *Isle*, and that is, the *Coast* of *Virginia*, being subject to gusts of *Winde*, the *Ships* loaden with *Goods* and *Passengers*, have been often forced forth to *Sea*, and so disabled, that they could not ply

Jamaica.

ply to any of the outward *Caribbee Islands*, but have been constrained to bear up, and put into the *Spanish Leeward Ports*; and likewise, some of our *Merchants* have been forced out of the *Caribbee Isles* by *Hurricane*'s (which are there common) and so disabled, that they could not keep *Sea*, but (as all *Vessels* thus distressed) have put into some of the *Spanish Leeward Ports*, where they have alwayes, been made *Prizes*. Now, *Jamaica* being so far *Leeward*, is a convenient *Harbour* for all *Vessels* thus distressed; and did some few years since save Three *Virginia Ships* full of *Passengers* and *Goods*, and formerly others; as also some driven by *Hurricanes* from the *Windward Islands*: All which, without the conveniency, and assistance of this *Isle*, had perished.

Barbadoes

A DESCRIPTION OF The ISLAND of BARBADOES.

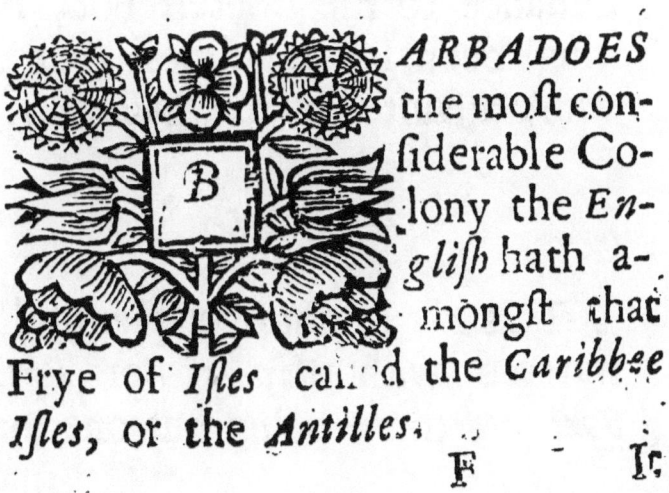ARBADOES the most considerable Colony the *English* hath amongst that Frye of *Isles* called the *Caribbee Isles*, or the *Antilles*.

Barbadoes.

Its Scituation.

Its Scituation.

It is seated in the North *Latitude* of 13 degrees, and 20 *min.* and although but of a small *circuit*, (being accounted not above 8 *Leagues* in length, and 5 in breadth where broadest, being of an Oval *Form*) yet is it a potent Colony, being able as occasion requireth, to arm 10000 Fighting men, which, with the strength that nature hath bestowed on it, it is able to bid defiance to the stoutest Foe, having been several times (but in vain) assaulted by the *Spaniards*.

Its Rivers.

Rivers.

This *Isle* is not over-plentifully watered with *Rivers*, or *Fresh Springs*, there being but one that may

Barbadoes. 67

may appropriate to it self that *Name*, or rather a *Lake*, which runneth not far into the *Land*; yet notwithstanding, the *Inhabitants* are not destitute thereof, for the Countrey lying low, and for the most part even, there are several *Pools* or *Ponds*; besides, most *Houses* have *Wells* or *Cisterns* which are always supplyed with Rain-water.

Here is also a *River*, which the *Inhabitants* call the *Tuigh*-River, from the top of whose *waters* is gathered an *Oyl*, which serveth them to burn in *Lamps*.

Its Fertility.

This *Isle* is exceeding Fertile, bearing Crops all the year long, and its *Trees* being always cloathed in their Summer Livery, and

Its Fertility.

F 2   the

the *Fields* and *Woods* in their Verdure, renders it very delightful to the *Inhabitants*. But the two principal seasons of the year for Planting, is in *May*, and *November*, but the *Sugar-Canes* are planted all the year round, the making of which, is not only very chargeable, but also as dangerous, and subject to casualties, either in the *Boyling-house*, with the *Coppers* and *Furnaces*; in the *Filling-room*, in the *Still-house*, or in the *Cureing-house*.

Its Commodities.

Commodities.   The *Commodities* that this *Isle* produceth, are *Sugars*, (which though not so white as those of *Brazile*, yet better when refined, being of a fairer grain) *Indico, Cotten, Wool, Ginger, Logwood, Fustick,*

stick, and *Lignum-vitæ*. And these *Commodities*, especially *Sugar*, *Indico*, *Cotton*, and *Ginger*, are here in such great abundance, that about 200 sayl of *Ships* and *Vessels*, both great and small, have yearly their loading; which after Imported in the several Ports of *England*, and *Ireland*, is again in great quantities exported to Forreign parts, to our great enrichment; and the rather, for that they are not permitted to *Trade* with any other Nation but the *English*, and such of his Majesties *Subjects* in *New-England*, *Virginia*, and *Bermudoes*: And in exchange of those *Commodities*, they take such as are necessary for the use of man, as well for the *Back* and *Belly*, as for their *Houses*, and *Plantations*; with many of which, they are supplyed from *New-England*,

land, *Virginia*, and the *Bermudoes*; together with *Servants*, and *Slaves*, as I have noted at the latter end of the description of *Jamaica*, about *page* 73. together with several sorts of *Commodities* and *Provisions*, which *Jamaica* hath no occasion of, as *Horses*, *Camels*, *Assinegroes*, *Cattel*; also salted *Flesh* and *Fish* of several sorts; *Butter* and *Cheese*; but by reason of the great heat of the weather, it will soon stink, and become unfit to eat; so that instead of *Butter*, they make great use of *Oyl* for their Sauces.

<small>Dayes & Nights almost equal.</small>

The *Dayes* and *Nights* are almost thorowout the *Year*, of an equal length, the Sun Rising and Setting at 6. except about *October*, and then there is some small difference.

The

The Temperature of Air.

This *Isle* is very *hott*, especially for 8 *months*, yet not so, but that Travel, and Labour is sufferable; but were it not for the cool *breezes* of *Winde* which Riseth with the *Sun*, and bloweth fresher as the Sun mounteth up, it would be unsufferable. And these *Breezes* always blow from *North-East*, and by *East*, unless it be in the time of the *Turnado*, and then for a few hours it chopps into the *South*, but returns to the same point again. And it is observed, that although the people do so much sweat, yet they have not that faintness as with us, in the months of *July* and *August*; neither are they so thirsty, without occasioned by excess of *Labour*, or *Drinking* of strong

strong *Liquors*, which the *People* are here too much addicted unto, to their great hurt, which if moderately taken, would be as great a preservative to comfort their inward parts, which are left cold, and faint, through their sweating. Besides, our bodies being accustomed to colder *Climates*, our spirits are not so vigorous without them in a moderate manner.

The Air moist. The *Air*, though hot, is very moist, which causeth all *Iron-tools*, as *Knives*, *Swords*, *Locks*, *Keys*, &c. to rust, so that without constant usage, they will soon become eaten up with rust. And this great *heat* and *moisture*, doth cause the *Plants* and *Trees* to grow so large, and high.

Barbadoes.

Their Fruits.

Here are abundance of *Fruits* of several sorts, as *Dates, Orenges* of two sorts, the one sweet, and the other sharp, *Pomgranates, Citrons, Limes, Lemons, Macows, Grapes, Juneper-Apples, Papayers, Momins, Monbains, Acajous, Icacos, Cherries, Raysins, Indian Figgs, Cocos, Plantins, Bonanoes, Guavers, Prickle-Apples, Prickle-Pears, Custard-Apples, Millons,* both land and water, and *Pine-Apples,* the rarest Fruit in the *Indies.*

Their Fish.

Here are great store of *Fish* in the *Sea,* as *Snappers, Crabs, Lobsters, Terbums, Macquerels, Mullots,*

lots, *Cavallos, Parrat-Fish, Cony-Fish*, and *green Turtles*, which of all others are the most delicious, with several other sorts appropriated to this and the rest of the *Caribbee Isles*. But the *Rivulets*, or *Ponds*, have few or no *Fish* in them.

Their Beasts.

Their Beasts. Here are no *Beasts* or *Cattel* but what are Tame, and brought them; as Camels, Horses, Assinegroes, Oxen, Bulls, Cowes, Sheep, and Goats, and Hoggs, which are here in great plenty in every *Plantation*, it being their common food, whose Flesh is esteemed very good and delicious; but as for *Beef*, and *Mutton*, it is very dear, as having but a small stock, but might be soon encreased, would they spare ground

Barbadoes. 75

ground enough for Pasturage for them from their other occasions.

Their Herbs and Roots.

Here groweth divers sorts of *English hearbs*, and *roots*, as *Rosemary, Lavender, Lavender-Cotton, Marjerom, Winter-Savory, Time, Parsley, Tansey, Sage, Purcelane*, &c. and for *Roots, Cabages, Colworths, Collyflowers, Turnips, Potatoes, Onyons, Garlick, Radishes, Lettice, Taragon, Marigolds*, &c.

Herbs, & Roots.

Their Birds and Fowles.

Here are several sorts of *Fowles*, as *Turkeys, Hens, Muscovy-ducks, Pigeons, Turtle-Doves*, &c. and for small *Birds*, great variety; as *Thrushes, Black-birds, Sparrows*, &c.

Birds and Fowles.

Their

Barbadoes.

Their Insects and Animals.

Animals, and Insects.

Here are several *Animals*, and *Insects*, as *Snakes* a yard and a half long, *Scorpions* as big as Rats, but no wayes hurtful to man or beast; *Lizzards*, which are exceeding harmless, much frequenting the houses, and loving the company of men; *Musketoes*, *Cockroches*, and *Merriwings*, which are very troublesome in the night in stinging; also, here are *land-Crabs* in great abundance, which are found good to eat. And here is a small Fly which they call *Cayouyou*, whose *Wings* in the Night, as it flyeth, casts forth a great lustre, and the *Indians* do commonly catch them, and tye them to their hands or feet, and make use of them instead of a *Candle*, which is forbidden them.

Their Trees.

Here are great variety of *Trees*, fit for several uses, as the *Locust*, *Mastick*, *Red-wood*, the *prickled-Yellow-wood*, the *Ironwood-Tree*, and the *Cedar* Tree, which are fit for building. Also, the *Cassia*, *Fistula*, *Coloquintida*, *Tamarine*, *Cassavie*, of which is made their bread; the *Poyson-Tree*, and the *Phisick-Nut*, these have a *Physical*, and some a *poysonous Vertue* in them. Also, here are these *Trees* following, the *Calibash*, the *Shell* of whose *Fruit*, serveth to carry liquid things in, being of the nature of *Goards*; the *Mangrass-Tree*, which is of an exceeding greatness; the *Roucou*, of whose *bark* is made *Ropes*, as also *Flax*, which being spun, is employed to several

ral uses; the *Lignum-vitæ*, the *Palmeto*, which is very large, and beautiful to behold; with several others.

Several Caves.

Several Caves. In this *Island* are divers *Caves*, some of which are very deep, and large enough to hold 500 *men*; and these *Caves* are often the Sanctuaries of such *Negro-slaves* that run away, in which they ofttimes lie a good while ere found out, seldome stirring in the day-time, although they are such unwholesome places, by reason of the great damps that are found in them. And it is supposed, that these *Caves* were the *Habitations* of the *Natives*.

Barbadoes.

Its Division and Towns.

This *Island* is severed into Eleven *Precincts*, or *Parishes*, in which are 14 *Churches* and *Chappels*, and here are many places which may not unaptly be called *Townes*, as being composed of a long and spacious Street, which are beautified with fair houses; and indeed the whole *Isle* for these many years, is so taken up with *Planters* (there being no wast ground to be found) that it is thorowout beset with *Houses*, at no great distance from one another.

Its Division, and Townes.

Its chief Townes.

1. St. *Michaels* formerly called the *Bridg-Town*, or *Indian-Bridg*, scituate at the bottome of *Carlisle-Bay*,

St. Michaels.

Barbadoes.

Bay in the *Leeward*, or Southern part of the *Isle*, which *Bay* is very capacious, deep, and secure for *Ships*, being large enough to entertain 500 *Vessels* at one time. The *Town* is long, containing several *Streets*, and graced with abundance of well-built houses. It is very populous, being the Residence of the *Governour*, or his *Deputy*, the place of *Judicature*, and the *Scale* of *Trade*, where most of the *Merchants*, and *Factors* in the *Isle* have their *Storehouses* for the negotiation of their *Affairs*; and from these *Storehouses* or *Shops*, the *Inhabitants* are supplyed with such *Commodities* as they have occasion of, in exchange of theirs, which are the product of of the *Isle*. The Town is ill seated, the ground being lower than the banks of the *Sea*, by which

means

Barbadoes.

means the Spring-*Tides* doth flow over, and there remaining, doth make a kind of of a moorish bogg, which doth occasion it to be more unhealthful than the other parts of the *Isle*. This Town for its defence, and security of the *Ships*, hath two strong Forts opposite to each other, with a *Platform* in the midst, which also commands the *Road*, all which are well Fortifyed with great Guns, &c. The principal of these *Forts* is called *Charles Fort*, being seated on *Nedhams Point*.

2. Little *Bristol*, formerly *Sprights Bay*, scituate about four Leagues Leeward from St. *Michaels*, hath a commodious Road for *Ships*, is a place well frequented, and traded unto, and is strongly Defended by two powerful Forts.

Litle Bristol.

3. St. *James*, formerly called the *Hall*, seated not far from *Bristol*, hath the accommodation of a good Road for *Ships*, and is a place of a considerable *Trade*, for its defence, besides a large *Platform*, hath fortified *Breast-works*; and in this *Town* is kept for the Precinct, the monthly *Courts*.

Charles-Town. 4. *Charles-Town*, seated windeward of St. *Michaels*, about two *Leagues*: And on *Oyster-Bay*, it is secured by two strong *Forts*, the one to the Windward, and the other to the Leeward, of the *Town* and *Road*, with a *Platform* in the midst. This *Town* hath the accomodation of weekly *Markets*, and here is kept the monthly *Courts* for the *Precinct*.

The other *Parishes* are of less note.

Other Places on the Sea-Coast.

Other Places of Name along the Sea-Coast of this *Isle*, begining Easterly, and so encompassing the *Isle*, are as followeth:

Fowl-Bay, *Austins-Bay*, *Maxwells-Bay*, where there is a small Isle, *Blackrock*, The *Hole*, *Spikes-Bay*, *Balises-Bay*, *Long-Bay*, *Clarks-Bay*, and *Constance-Bay*.

The Inhabitants.

The *Inhabitants* of this *Isle* may be Ranged under 3 heads or sorts, to witt, Masters, (which are *English*, *Scotch*, and *Irish*; with some few *Dutch*, *French*, and *Jews*) Christian Servants, and *Negro-Slaves*. And these three sorts are exceeding numerous; for, according to a Calculation not long since made, the *Masters*, and *Servants*, did amount to about 50000, and the *Negroes* to about double the number.

The *Masters*, for the most part, live at the height of Pleasure.

The *Servants*, at the expiration of 5 years, become Freemen of the *Island*, and employ their times according to their *abilities*, and *capacities*; either to get a small *Plantation*, or to *work* at day-labour in other *Plantations*, or else to exercise their *Trades*, if so capacitated.

N. gro-Slaves. The *Negro-Slaves* are never out of their *Bondage*, and the *Children* they get, are likewise perpetual *Slaves*. They have but mean allowance of *dyet*, *cloaths*, and *lodging*; and although held to such hard Labour, and so ill treated, yet

Barbadoes.

yet are they well contented with their *Conditions*; and if their *Master* is but any thing kind, they think nothing too much to be done for them; and therefore 'tis great pity to wrong such poor *Creatures*.

The chiefest *Stock* of a *Planter*, consists in his *Servants* and *Slaves*, but especially the *Slaves*, who are more numerous. And these they Buy on *Shipboard*, as men Buy Horses in a *Fayr*, and according as they are handsome, lusty, well-shapen, and young, either the *men* or *women*, they give more or less; the general Rates for the Christian-servants being about 10*l*. but if one that hath a good Trade, as a *Carpenter*, *Joyner*, *Smith*, or the like, then far more: Likewise, a Female that is young and handsome, is higher valued. The general Rate for the better sort of

Negro-men, is 20*l.* or 25*l.* sterling; and for *Women*, about 15*l.* for the encrease of stock of *Negroes*, they generally take as many *Men* as *Women*.

The Maintenance of the Servants and Slaves.

The Maintenance of the *Servants*, and *Negro-Slaves*, as to their Dyet, Apparel, and Lodging, is very inconsiderable.

Their Food. For their *Food*, they are contented from weeks-end, to weeks-end, with *Potatoes*, *Loblolly*, made of beaten *Maize* mixt with water; *Caſſader-bread* common in all the *Indies*, *Bonaviſt*, and such like food that the *Plantation* affordeth; as for *Meat*, they are seldome troubled with it, except at *Chriſtmas*, *Eaſter*, and *Whitſontide*, and then

Barbadoes.

they have *Hoggs-flesh*, according to the custome of the *Island*; but of late, the servants are allowed weekly, a small quantity of *Swines-Flesh*, or salted *Flesh*, or *Fish*; and when any of the *Cattle* dye of any distemper, or by accident, it is given to the *Negroes*, who feed like Princes on it.

Their *Drinks* are *Mobbie*, made of *Potatoes* soaked in water; *Perino*, made of *Casavie-Root* and water; *Crippo*, *Kill-Devil*, *Punch*, made of water and Sugar; *Plantin-drink*, made of *Plantins* and water; *Beveridge*, made of Spring-water, *Sugar*, and the juyce of *Orenges*; and *wine* of *Pines*, which is only made of the juyce of the *Fruit*, which is exceeding good and delicious; but this sort, as also the *Beveridge*, and *Punch*, the servants are not much troubled with.

Their Drink.

But as for the *Master-Planters*, *Merchants*, *Factors*, and *Strangers*, their Faire is far otherwise, having their curious-made *Dishes*, as *Custards*, *Cheese-cakes*, *Tansies*; also, *Sturgeon*, *Anchoves*, *Caviare*, *Botardo*, *Neates-Tongues*, besides *Poultrey*, *Fish*, *Fowl*, *Mutton*, *Beef*, *Kid*, *Porke*, *Beans*, *Pease*, several *Roots*, and other good *Dishes*. And, besides the several sorts of *Liquors* already named, *Wines*, *Strong waters*, *Brandy*, and *English-Beer*; so that they find no want, and do not consider the condition of those poor wretches, their *Servants* and *Slaves*, who are constrained to so hard a labour.

Their Apparel. The *Apparel* they allow their *Servants* yearly, for the men, are 6 pair of *Drawers*, 12 pair of *Shoos*, 3 *Monmouth-Caps*, 6 *Shirts*; and for the women, 4 *Smocks*, 3 *Petticoats*,

Barbadoes.

coats, 4. *Coifes*, and 12 paire of *Shoos*, besides, a Rug-Gown to each, to keep them warm, in the night, and to put on them when they come sweating from their labour. To the *Negro-men*, they allow but 3 pair of *Canvas-Drawers*, and to the *Women*, but three *Petticoats*.

But for themselves (especially the better sort) they are exceeding profuse and costly.

The *Lodging* of these poor wretches is worst of all, for having laboured all the day in so hot a *Countrey*, without any nourishing *Dyet*, at night they must be contented to lye hard, on nothing but a *board*, without any *Coverled*, in their *Hutts*, or rather *Hogsties*; but Christian *Servants* are something better Treated, being allowed *Hamocks*.

Their Lodging.

Every

Every *Sunday*, (which is the only day of Rest, and should be set apart for the service of God) they employ either in the getting of the Bark of *Trees*, and making of *Ropes* with it, which they Truck away for *Shirts*, *Drawers*, and the like; or else spend the day in Recreation, as *Dancing*, and *Wrestling*, which they much delight in, though they are no great Proficients in either; for in their *Dancing*, they use antick actions, their hands having more of motion than their feet; and their head, than either; nor do the men and women *Dance* together, but apart; the *Musique* to which they *Dance*, being a sort of *Kettle-drums*, one bigger than another, which makes a strange and various noise, but whither Harmonious, I leave to the judgment of the Reader.

Barbadoes.

It is thought by many, that the *Christians* should be in danger of being murthered by the *Negro-Slaves*, who so much over-top them in number, and the rather, for that they are so cruelly used, and for that reason, many are fearful to venture to dwell here. But this Objection may be thus answered; that first, they are such as were brought from several parts of *Affrica*, and do not understand one anothers Language; and then they are stir'd up with an inb-read hatred against one another, it being the custome in those parts, for several petty *Kings* to go to Wars against one another; and the *Prisoners* that are taken of each side, they sell unto us, and other *European Nations* that come to *Traffique* with them; also, they are not permitted to touch, nay, hardly to see

see a *Gun*, or any other *weapon*; and being kept in such a *slavery*, they are fearful of begining such an Insurrection, it being present death for any that shall in the least be found to act, or contrive such a thing.

The Management of a Plantation. The *Management* of a *Plantation*, ought to be the *Masters* care, yet few of them (except those of the meaner degree) are without their *Overseers*, who takes off that trouble from them, whose Office is to call them to work by the Ring of a *Bell*, at 6 a clock in the morning, to appoint them their several works, to give them due Correction upon any Misdemeanour, or Idleness; he likewise dismisses them at 11 a clock, to go to their Dinner, and calls them again by One a clock by the said Bell, and dischargeth them at 6 at night.

What

Barbadoes. 93

What I have said in this Treatise of *Barbadoes* concerning their *Servants*, and *Slaves*, may be said in that of *Jamaica*; for the *Servants*, and *Slaves*, are their greatest stock; those they Buy, the *Servants* for a Tearm of years, the *Negroes* for ever; their *Apparrel* which they allow to either being much the same, but their Dyet better; and for their labour, it may be said to be much the same, the *Island* producing the same *Commodities*.

The Island of Barbados *very strong.*

This *Island* is very strong, as well by *Nature* as *Art*, being sheltered with *Rocks*, and *Shoals*; and where nature hath not thus defended it, it is Fortified by *Trenches* and *Rampiers*, with *Pallisadoes*, Cur-

The Island very strong

Curtains, and *Counter-Scarfes*; besides, round about the *Isle*, re-guarding the *Sea*, is standing-*Wood*: Here are also, for its further Defence, 3 *Forts*, one for a *Magazine* for the *Ammunition*, and *Powder* to lye in, and the other two for places of *Retreats*, as occasion serveth. They have also for their further security, a standing *Militia*, consisting of two *Regiments* of *Horse*, and five of *Foot*, which are Stout, and well-Disciplined men, and always to be Ready on beat of Drum.

The Government of this Isle.

<small>The Government of the Island.</small>

This *Isle* is Governed by *Lawes* assimulated to those of *England*, for all matters either *Civil*, *Ecclesiastick*, *Criminal*, *Maritine*, or *Martial*; yet not without some few *Lawes* appropriate to themselves, which are not repugnant

to

Barbadoes.

to the *Lawes* of *England*.

For the Execution of these *Lawes*, they have their *Courts* of *Judicature*.

The *Law* is administred by the *Governour*, or his *Deputy*, and Ten of his *Council*.

The *Isle* is divided into four *Circuites*, in each of which, there is an Inferiour *Court* for civil *Causes*, from which, Appeals may be made to the *Supream Court*.

<small>The Isle divided into four Circuits.</small>

Here are also *Justices* of the Peace, *Constables*, *Church-wardens*, and *Tything-men*.

And for the *Administration* of *Justice*, here are yearly 5 *Sessions*.

At the *Governours* pleasure, he calleth an Assembly for the making of New *Lawes*, (so, as not contrary to those of *England*) and for the abolishing of Old; which said *Assembly* is much in the nature

nature of our *Parliament*, and doth consist of the *Governour* as *Supream*, his Ten Council as so many *Peers*, and two *Burgesses*, chosen by the Commonalty out of each of the *Parishes*.

<small>The present Governour.</small> The present Governour is the Right Hon. *William Willoughby*, Baron *Willoughby* of *Parham*.

As concerning the nature of the *Sugar-Canes*, how to *Plant* them, their *growth, cutting, grinding, boyling*; the *conveyance* of the *Skimmings* into the *Cisterns*, how to *distill* it for *Spirits*; how long it stayes in the *Cureing-house*, before it be good *Muscovado-Sugar*; together with the making it into *Whites*, is not my business in this small *Treatise*, to give the Reader <small>See Mr. Ligons Book of Barbadoes page 87.</small> instructions therein, referring to Mr. *Richard Ligons* Book of the Description of this *Isle*.

A DESCRIPTION OF The ISLAND of St. CHRISTOPHERS.

ST. *Christophers*, so called from *Christopher Columbus*, the first discoverers thereof, scituate in the *Latitude* of 17 degrees, and 25 *min.* in circuite, about 75 *miles*: The Land lieth high and mountainous in the midst, from which springeth several *Rivers*, —Its Scituation, &c.

vers, which oft-times, by reason of the *Raines* that falleth down the *Mountaines*, are overflown to the detriment of the *Inhabitants*.

The Soyl, Commodities, &c.

Its Soyl, and Commodities

The *Soyl* is light and sandy, and very apt to produce several sorts of *Fruits, Provisions*, and *Commodities*; as *Sugar, Tobacco, Cotton, Ginger*, &c.

This *Isle*, by reason of its several great and steepy *Mountains*, between which, are Springs of hot, and Sulphurous *Water*, with horrid *Precipices*, and thick *Woods*, renders it very impassable through the midst: And the steepy *Ascents* of the *Mountains*, are divided into several *Stages*, or *Stories*, where are spacious wayes.

On

On the *Sea-side* there is a *Salt-pit* called *Gul-desac*, and not far from the said *Salt-pit*, there is a small *Istmus* of land, which reacheth within a mile and a half of the Island of *Nievis*, or *Mevis*.

This *Island* is a place exceeding delightful, and of a most delectable Prospect to the Eye of the beholder; for if the Eye be directed downwards, from the top, it hath a Prospect of curious *Gardens*, which gently descend to the Seaside; and in reguard of the continual Ascent of the *Isle*, the lower *Stage* or *Story*, doth not debar the *Eye* of the pleasant Prospect of that which lyeth at a Remoter distance, which is terminated by those high *Mountains*: And that which maketh the Prospect the more delectable in the several *Plantations* (which are bounded with

The Isle very delightful, and of a pleasing Prospect.

with Rows of *Trees* alwayes in their Verdure) are the fair *Houses* covered with glazed Slate.

The Division of the Isle, and how Possessed.

The Isle Possessed by the English, & French

The whole *Isle* is divided into four *Quarters* or *Cantons*, two of which, are possessed by the *English*, and two by the *French*; which parts are not so well watered, as those of the *English*, but are better for *Tillage*, and not so *Hilly*.

The *English* are more Populous then the *French*, and have two fortified places, one commanding the great *Haven*, and the other a descent not far from *Pointe de sable*.

The *French* have Four strong *Forts*, of which one hath *Regular Works* like a *Cittadel*, that of most note commands the *Haven*, and is called *Baſſe-Terre*.

Both the *Engliſh*, and the *French*, keep conſtant Guard at their *Forts*, placed at the entrance of the *Paths* which leads to the ſeveral *Wards*, for the better ſecurity of each other.

Here are five *Churches* in thoſe parts belonging to the *Engliſh*, viz. one at *Sandy-point*, one at *Palme-Tree*, another near the great Road, and two at the Inlet of *Cayoune*, with many fair Structures. {Their Churches.}

The *French*, beſides their ſeveral *Habitations*, diſperſed up and down in their *quarters*, have at *Baſſe-Terre* (near the *Haven* where *Ships* lye at Anchor) a *Town* of a good bigneſs, whoſe *Houſes* are well built, of *Brick*, *Freeſtone*, and *Timber*; where the *Merchants* have their *Store-houſes*, and is well {A Town Poſſeſſed by the French}

H 3 In-

Inhabited by *Tradesmen*, and are well served with such *Commodities*, both for the *Back*, and *Belly*, together with *Utensils* for their *Houses*, and *Plantations*, as they have occasion of, in exchange of such *Commodities* which are the product of the *Island*. Here is a fair, and large *Church*, as also a *publique-Hall*, for the administration of *Justice*: Here is also a very fair *Hospital*, built by the *General*, for such people that cannot get cure at their *Houses*; where they are well maintained and attended by *Doctors*, and *Physitians*, for the recovery of their Healths. Here is also a stately *Castle*, being the Residence of the *Governour*, most pleasantly seated, at the foot of a high *Mountain*, not far from the *Sea*, having spacious *Courts*, delightful *Walks*, and *Gardens*, and enjoyeth a curious prospect.   A

A DESCRIPTION OF The ISLAND of NIEVIS, or MEVIS.

THe Island of *Nievis*, or *Mevis*, lyeth not far from St. *Christophers*, as I have before noted, and in the *Latitude* of Seventeen degrees, and Nineteen *minutes*. — *Its Scituation.*

It is but small, being not above Eighteen miles in Circuite. — *Extent.*

There

There is but One *Mountain* in the *Isle*, and that is seated in the midst, which is of a great height, but of an easy Access, and cloathed with *Trees* from its Somett to the bottom; and about this Mountain, are the *Plantations* which reach to the *Sea-Shore*.

Springs of Water.

<small>A Spring of Mineral water, and Baths.</small>

Here are divers *Springs of Fresh-Water*, and one Spring of a *Hott* and *Mineral Water*; not far from whose Spring-head are *Baths* made, which are much frequented for the curing of several distempers of the Body of man.

It is indifferent Fertile, and hath store of Deer, and other Game for *Hunting*.

The

Nevis.

The *Isle* is Inhabited by about three or four Thousand; who live well, and drive a *Trade* for such things as they have occasion for, by exchanging such *Commodities* as the *Isle* produceth; as, *Sugar, Cotton, Ginger, Tobacco,* &c.

It is a well-Governed *Colony,* where Justice is duly administred, and all Vices severely punished.

For the Worship of God, here are three *Churches;* and for its further defence, and safety, it hath a *Fort,* whereon are mounted several Peeces, for the security of the *Ships* in the Road, or Harbour, called *Bath-Bay,* as also the publique-Store-house. *(Their Churches, &c.)*

This *Isle,* as the rest of the *Caribbee's,* are troubled with
Mus-

Muſcheto's, *Chigos*, *Murigoins*, and other *Stinging Flyes*, which do much Annoy the Inhabitants.

A DESCRIPTION OF The ISLAND of ANTEGO.

THe *Island* of *Antego*, is seated in the *Latitude* of 16 degrees, and 11 *min*. *Its Scituation.*

It is in Length, about six, or seven Leagues, and about the same breadth in many places. *Extent.*

It is of a difficult acceſs, and very

very dangerous for *Shipping*, by reason of the Rocks which encompass it.

The Number of Inhabitants. It hath some few *Springs* of *Fresh-water*, besides which, the *Inhabitants*, which are about 8 or 900. have made several *Cisterns*, and *Ponds*, for the preserving of *Rain-Water*.

Fish. The *Isle* doth abound in *Fish*, amongst which, is the *Sword-Fish* which of all others, would be the chief in the *Sea*.

Fowl, & Cattle. Here are great plenty of most sorts of Wild Fowl, and not wanting in *Venison*, and Tame *Cattle*.

Commodities. The *Commodities* that it affordeth, are *Sugar*, *Indico*, *Ginger*, *Tobacco*, &c.

The Lord propriator of this *Isle* is, the Rt. Hon. *Will.* Ld. *Willowby* of *Parham*, who is Governour of the *Island* of *Barbadoes*, and some other *Isles*. A

A DESCRIPTION OF The ISLAND of St. *VINCENT*.

THE *Island* of St. *Vincent*, lyeth in the *Latitude* of Sixteen degrees. *Its Scituation.*

It is about 20 miles in length, and Fifteen in breadth, of a Fertile *Soyl*, yielding abundance of *Sugar-Canes*; which grow Naturally without Planting. *Extent, and Fertility.*

It

St. Vincent.

It is well watered with *Rivers*, and affordeth many safe *Roads*, and convenient *Bayes*, for *Shipping*.

The *English* have here some *Settlement*, but are not very powerful.

A DESCRIPTION OF The ISLAND of DOMINICA.

THis *Isle* is seated in the *La-*   Its Scitu-
titude of Fifteen degrees   ation,
and a half.

 It is about 12 *Leagues* Extent.
in length, and 8 in breadth.

 On the *West* side of the *Isle*,
there is a convenient Harbour for
Ships.

It

It is very *Montainous*, yet not without many Fertile *Valleys*, producing several *Commodities*; but chiefly *Tobacco*, which is planted by the *English*; but the *Natives* which are *Canibals*, and very Barbarous, doth much hinder the comming of the *English* to settle here.

A DESCRIPTION OF The ISLAND of MONTSERRAT.

MONTSERRAT, an *Island* of a small Extent, not exceeding *Ten miles* in Length, and of a less Breadth.

Its Extent, Scituation, Fertility, &c.

It is seated in the *Latitude* of 17 degree: It is much inclined to

Moun-

Mountains, which are well cloathed with *Cedar*, and other *Trees*; and the *Valleys*, and *Plains* are very Fertile.

This *Isle* is most Inhabited by the *Irish*, who have here a *Church* for Divine *Worship*.

A DESCRIPTION OF The ISLAND of ANGUILLA.

THis *Isle* is seated in the *La-* titude of Eighteen degrees, and One and Twenty *Minutes*.   *Its Scituation, extent, &c.*

It Extendeth it self in length, about Ten *Leagues*, and in breadth about Three.

Anguilla.

The *Inhabitants* are *English*, which are Computed to amount unto two or three Hundred, who are but poor, the *Isle* being said not to be worth the keeping.

A

A DESCRIPTION OF The ISLAND of BARBADA.

BARBADA, or *Barboude*, scituate in the *Latitude* of of Seventeen degrees and a half. *Its Scituation, Fertility, &c.*

It is an *Isle* of no great Extent, not exceeding Fifteen miles in Length, nor is it of any considerable Account to the *English*, who are the Possessors of it: Yet is it found to be of a Fertile Soyl, and to be well stored with *Cattle, Sheep,* &c. and may produce several good *Commodities,* were it well managed, to the advantage of the *Inhabitants.*

A DESCRIPTION OF The ISLES of BERMUDES, OR, The Summer-ISLES.

EAſt of *Virginia*, and *Caroli-* | Their
na, which is a part of *Flo-* | Scituati-
rida, lyeth the Iſles of *Ber-* | on, and
mudes, ſo called, from | Name.
John Bermudes a *Spaniard*, by

I 4 whom

whom they were first discovered. They are also called the *Summer-Isles*, from the *Shipwrack* that one *George Summers* (an *English*-man) there suffered.

These *Isles* lye distant from *England*, about 15 or 1600 *Leagues*, from *Madera*, 1000, or 1200; from *Hispaniola*, 400; and from *Carolina*, which is the neerest part of Land, about 300 *Leagues*.

Their Extent.

St. Georges Isle.
Of these *Isles*, the greatest called St. *Georges*, is 5 or 6 Leagues long, and almost thorowout, not above a quarter, a third, or half a League broad, the others are much less.

Their Form, &c.

All these *Isles* together, form a body

Bermudes.

body like a *Cressent*, and inclose very good *Ports*, the chief among which, are those of the *Great-Sound, Herringtons Inlet, South-hampton,* and *Pagets*; which, with their *Forts* of *Dover*, and *Warwick*, take their names from the several Noble men that were concerned as undertakers.

<small>Several good Ports:</small>

The Fertility, Commodities, Fruits, &c.

The *Earth* is exceeding Fertile, yeilding two Crops yearly; their *Maize* they gather in *July*, and *December*.

<small>Its Fertility.</small>

They have excellent *Fruits*, as, *Oranges, Dates, Mulberries* both White and Red; where breed abundance of *Silk-worms* which spin *Silk.*

<small>Their Fruits.</small>

Their chief *Commodities* are, O-ranges

Their Commodities. *Oranges*, *Couchaneil*, and *Tobacco*, with some *Pearl*, and *Amber-greece*, and with these they drive some small *Trade*.

They have plenty of *Tortoises*, which is their ordinary food, whose *Flesh* is very delicious.

Hoggs. Their *Hoggs*, which the *Spaniards* formerly carried thither, are greatly encreased.

Fowles. They have many *Fowles*, and *Birds*, amongst which, a great many *Cranes*, with a *Sea-Fowl* that breeds in holes like *Rabbets*.

Defective in Fresh-water. They have no *Fresh-Water* for their occasions, but that of *Wells*, and *Pits*, which *Ebbs* and *Flowes* with the *Sea*, there being neither *Fountain* nor *Stream* in these *Isles*.

No Venemous Beast.

In these *Isles* are no *Venemous Beast*,

beast, their *Spiders* are not poy-   Their
sonous, but are of sundry and va-   Spiders.
rious *Colours*; and in the hot weather, they make their *Webs* so
strong, that oft-times the small
Birds are entangled and catched in
them.

Cadar Trees.

Here are *Cadar Trees*, which
differs from all others in several re-
spects, but the wood is very sweet.

The Air and Healthfulness.

The *Skie* is almost always Se-   These
rene, and when darkned with   Isles ex-
clouds, it commonly *Thunders*, and   healthful
Lightneth: And the *Air* is very
Temperate, and so exceeding
healthful, that it is rare to hear
that any one dyeth of any Distemper,

per, but only Old age; insomuch, that many have removed from *England* hither, only for the enjoyment of a long, and healthful life. And those that have made any long continuance here, are fearful of removing out of so pure an *Air*.

The Inhabitants.

<small>The Inhabitants and strength of the Ile.</small>

The *English* first setled themselves on these *Isles* about the year 1612. and have now established a powerful *Colony*, there being at present, about four or five Thousand *Inhabitants*, who have strongly Fortified the *Approaches*, which with the *Rocks* in the *Sea*, renders them Impregnable.

A

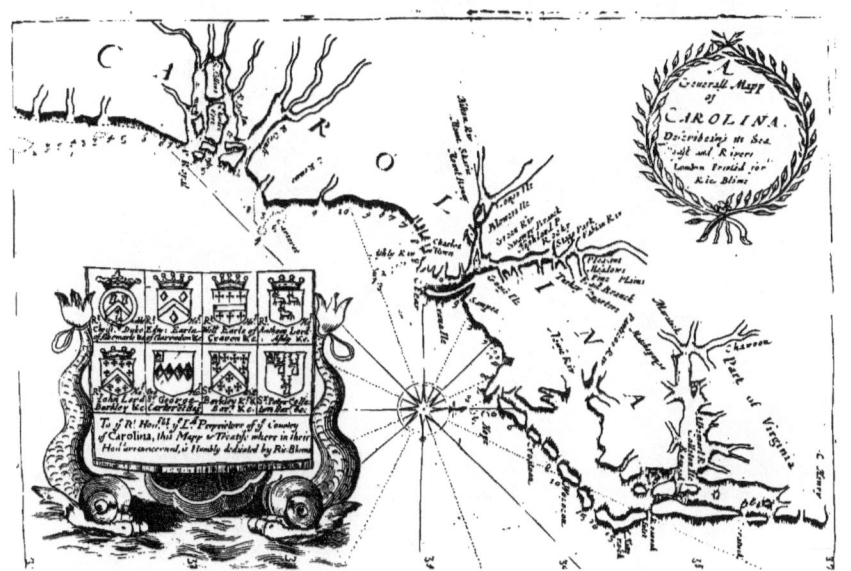

A DESCRIPTION OF CAROLINA.

CAROLINA, a New established *Colony*, of the *English*, being that part of *Florida* adjoyning to *Virginia*, which makes its Northern bounds in the *Latitude* of 36 degrees; and extendeth it self to the *Latitude* of 29, which makes its extream Southern bounds; on the East it is washed with the *Atlantick Ocean*, and

Its Bounds, and Scituation.

and on the West, it hath that large Tract of land which runneth into the *Pacifique Ocean*.

Its Temperature, and Healthfulness.

<small>This Country very healthful.</small>

It is a *Countrey* blest with a Temperate, and Wholesome *Air*, the *heat* in *Summer*, nor the *Cold* in *Winter*, which is not so much as to check the growth of Plants, Trees, &c. The several Fruits, and Plants, having their distinct seasons, being no wayes offensive to the *Inhabitants*. Neither is the *Air* thus Temperate, and Agreeable, to the *Natives* only, but it is as Favourable to the *English*: And being thus healthful, hath Invited several persons from the *Bermudes* to settle here; who dwelling in so pure an *Air*, durst not venture in any other *Countrey*. Nor do do those from the *Bermudes* only remove hither, upon the assurance of a happy life, joyned with the gaining of Fair *Estates*, but also, many *English* from most of the *American Plantations*, it being generally esteemed one of the best *Colonies* that ever the *English* were Masters of; for here is *Health*, *Pleasure*, and *Profit* to be found, which cannot be met with in so large a measure, in any *Countrey* of the *Indies*.

Their Fruits, Hearbs, &c.

The *Soyl* is Rich, and Fertile, and produceth excellent *Fruits*, as *Apricocks*, *Peaches*, *Grapes*, (of which the *English* have made good *Wine*) *Olives*, *Walnuts*, *Apples*, *Pears*, *Plumbs*, *Cherries*, *Figgs*, *Mulberries*, *Strawberries*,

Their Fruits.

water-

Water-Mellons, Marachocks, Quinces, and other *Fruits* known to us in *Europe,* which for goodness are no wayes Inferiour to them; and in the Southern part, *Oranges, Limes, Pomgranates,* and *Pome-Citrons.* And indeed, the Earth is very apt to produce, and bring to Maturity, *Corn,* all sorts of *Garden-Herbs,* and *Roots,* &c.

Its Commodities.

Commodities. The *Commodities* which this *Countrey* doth, and may produce, are *Wines, Oyls, Silk,* (*Mulberry-Trees* growing in great abundance in the *Woods*) *Cotton, Indico, Ginger, Tobacco,* &c. And it is believed, that here may be made of the three first *Commodities,* viz. *Wines, Oyl,* and *Silk,* in such great abundance, to theirs, and this

Kingdoms enrichment, that besides what we shall use our selves, we may have wherewith to furnish *Forrain Parts.*

Their Trees.

Besides the *Mulberry-Trees*, here are those of *Cædar, Oak*, both White and Red, *Poplar, Bay, Ash*, and *Pine*; with several others whose names are yet unknown.

<small>Trees.</small>

Their Rivers, Fish, and Fowl.

The *Countrey* is very well watered with *Rivers*, there being between *Cape-Carteret*, and *Port-Rasal*, which is not above 60 *miles*, 5 or 6 great Navigable *Rivers*, which discharge themselves into the *Sea*, besides several others of less Remark. And these *Rivers* are

<small>Rivers.</small>

K   plen-

plentifully stored with excellent *Fish* of sundry sorts, which being the same as are found in *Virginia*, which comes next to be treated of, I shall omit the nameing of them here.

Their Fowles.   Here are also great plenty of *Wild-Fowl*, as *Geese, Cranes, Swans, Herons, Curlews, Heath-Cocks, Oxeys, Brants, Dotterels, Widgeons, Teals,* and *Duck,* and *Mallard* in an undestroyable quantity.

Provisions in the Woods.

The *Woods* are well stored with large *Turkeys, Phesants, Partridges, Turtle-Doves, Wood-Pidgeons,* with great variety and plenty of small *Birds.* Also in the *Woods,* are great plenty of *Deer,* with abundance of *Hares, Coneys,* &c.

Here

Here are divers delightful, and spacious *Savanas*.

The Natives of Carolina.

The *Natives* of *Carolina*, according to the obſervation of Mr. *John Ledener* (who made three ſeveral journeys from *Virginia*, to *Carolina*, about the year 1670. on purpoſe for a diſcovery of thoſe parts, and the better underſtanding the nature and diſpoſition of the *Inhabitants*) are ſaid by him, to be a people of a ready witt, and though Illiterate, of a good underſtanding. For the *Account* of *time*, (he ſaith,) they make uſe of *Hieroglyphicks*, and *Emblems* of *things*; likewiſe they inſtruct their *Children* in ſuch things as relates to their *Families* and *Countrey*, which is ſo preſerved from *Generation*, to

The Diſpoſition, &c. of the Natives.

Generation; where a battle hath been fought, or upon the settlement of a *Colony*, they raise a small *Pyramid* of stone, which doth consist of the number *slain*, or setled at such a *Colony*. For *Religious Rites*, either *Devotion*, *Sacrifice*, or *Burial*, they make a round circle of short *Strawes*, or *Reeds*, and according to the placing of the said *Strawes*, or *Reeds*, it is known for what it was made; and to meddle with such *Circles*, is esteemed no better than *Sacriledge*.

He saith, they worship one *God*; as *Creator* of all *things*, to whom their *High-Priest* offers *Sacrifice*, but believes he hath somthing else to do, than to reguard *Humane Affairs*, but doth commit the Government thereof to lesser *Deities*; that is, to *good* and *evil Spirits*, to whom their Inferiour *Priests* makes

makes their *Devotion*, and *Sacrifice*. He saith, they beleive the *Transmigration* of the *Soul*, and when any one dyeth, they Interr with the *Corps*, *Provisions*, and *Housholdstuff* for the *Elizium* or next *World*, which they fancy to be beyond the *Mountains*, and *Indian Ocean*. He further saith, that from four women, they believe all mankind Sprung, and do therefore divide themselves into as many *Tribes*; and in their *Marriages*, they are very Superstitious.

He saith, they are generally well-proportionate; they are great Favourers of the *English*, living together in Love and Friendship, and upon all occasions, ready to contribute their assistance unto them. They are generally of a good, and honest meaning, no wayes addicted to *Vice*, or to *Extra-*

Extravagancies, contenting themselves with a mean *Dyet* and *Apparrel* for their present subsistance, not taking much care for the time to come. He further saith, that they are much addicted to *Mirth*, and *Dancing*; they are also much prone to *Honour*, and *Valour*, which they place above all other *Vertues*, which doth occasion them to be so continually engaged against one another in Wars: and that side which Fortune Crowneth with Victory, Triumphal *Follaties* are performed by them.

Its Division into Kingdomes. The *Countrey* (he saith) is divided into several petty *Kingdoms*, and the *People* in the one, keep no good Correspondence with those that border upon them, and on the least occasion, wage *War* one against another.

In this *Countrey* of *Carolina* (he saith)

Carolina.

saith) that there are several *Indian Towns* which are generally the Habitation of the *King*, that commands the *Territory*.

The Proprietors of Carolina.

This *Province* or *Countrey* of *Carolina*, was first Possessed by the *English*, about the year 1660, and became a *Proprietorship*; which his present *Majesty* K. *Charles* the Second, granted by Patent to the Right Noble, *George* Duke of *Albemarle*, Earl of *Torrington*, Baron *Moncke* of *Potheridge, Peachampe* and *Teys*, Knight of the Noble Order of the *Garter*, Captain General of his Majesties *Land-Forces*, and one of the Lords of his Majesties most Honourable Privy *Council*, &c. The Right Honourable, *Edward* Earl of *Clarendon*,

rendon, Viscount *Cornbury*, and Baron *Hide* of *Hendon*, &c. The Right Honourable, *William* Earl of *Craven*, Viscount *Craven* of *Uffington*, Baron *Craven* of *Hamsted-Marshal*, Lord Lieutenant of the County of *Middlesex*, and Borouh of *Southwark*, and one of the Lords of his Majesties most Honourable *Privy Council*, &c. The Right Honourable *John* Lord *Berkley*, Baron *Berkley* of *Stratton*, Lord Lievtenant of *Ireland* for his Majesty, &c. The Right Honourable, *Anthony* Lord *Ashley*, Baron *Ashley* of *Winbourn* St. *Giles*, *Chancellour* of the *Exchequor*, *under-Treasurer* of *England*, one of the Lords *Commissioners* of the *Treasury*, and one of the Lords of his Majesties most Honourable *Privy Council*, &c. The Honourable Sr. *George Carteret* of *Hawnes*

nes in *Bedfordshire* Baronet, *Vice-Chamberlain* of his Majesties *Houshold*, and one of his Majesties most Honourable *Privy Council*, &c. Sr. *William Berkley* of in the County of Knight and Baronet, and to Sr. *John Colleton* of *London*, Knight and Baronet; and to their *Heirs* and *Successors*.

And the said *Lords proprietors*, having by their *Patent*, power to establish a *Government*, and make *Lawes* for the better Regulation thereof, and the inviting of *Inhabitants*, have formed a *Model*, (which by the general consent of all the *Proprietors*) was drawn up by the Right Honourable the Lord *Ashley*, a person of great Worth, and Prudence; whose knowledg in matters of *State*, and the *Settlement* of a *Government*, is sufficiently

ently praise worthy by all persons. Which said *Model* is so well framed, for the good and welfare of the *Inhabitants*, that it is esteemed by all judicious persons without compare; but the said *Model*, being too long to be set down in this small Treatise, I must be constrained to omit it.

The Settlements of the English.

Here are at present two considerable Settlements of the *English*, for so short a time, the one at *Albemarle*-River in the *North*, and the other about the midst of the *Countrey* on *Ashley River*, which is likely to be the *Scale* of Trade for the whole Countrey, as being scituate very Commodious for Shipping, and in a healthful place.

A

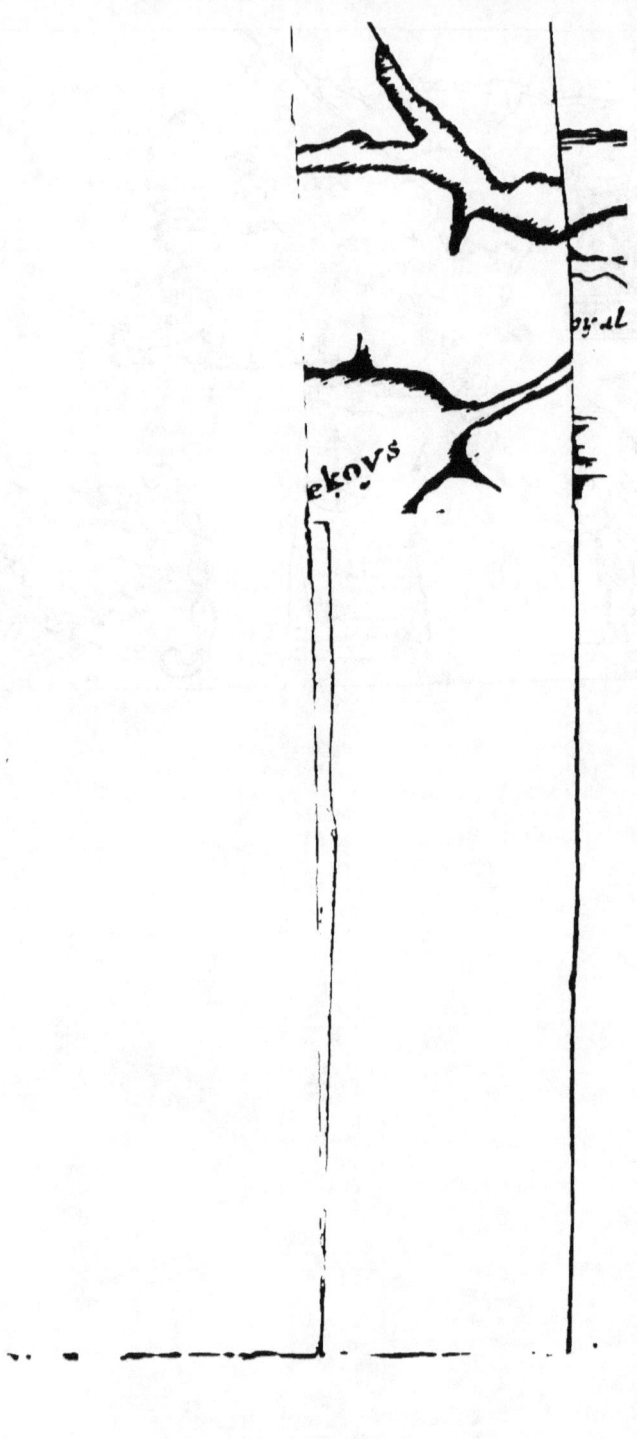

A DESCRIPTION OF VIRGINIA.

Its Bounds.

VIRGINIA particularly now so called, hath for its Southern Limits, *Carolina*; for its Eastern, the *Atlantick* Ocean; for its Northern, *Mariland*; and for its Western, that vast tract of *Land* which runneth into the *South-Sea*.

Virginia.

Its Name.

Its Name and why so called.

This *Countrey* was said to be first discovered by Sr. *Francis Drake* (as indeed all this Tract of Sea-Coast) and was so named by Sir. *Walter Rawleigh*, (a great promoter of this discovery,) in honour of Queen *Elizabeth*, who then Reigned.

The Settlement of the English.

† *Capt. Smith, a great Promoter of the English setling at Virginia.*

Much time was spent in the discovery of this *Countrey*, with vast expences in the setting forth of *Ships*, and not without the great loss of many a poor wretches life, before it could be brought to perfection; but at length, through the Industry of † Captain *John Smith*, and other worthy persons, who took great pains

Virginia. 141

pains for the advancement of these discoveries, fortune began to smile on her, and about the Reign of King *James*, a *Patent* was granted to certain persons as a *Corporation*, and called the Company of *Adventurers* of *Virginia*. Afterwards other *Patents* were granted to them for larger Extents of *Land* excluded in the former; but the said *Corporation* committing of several, and frequent Misdemeanours, and Miscarriages, the said *Patent* about the year 1623 was made *Nul*; since which it hath been free for all his *Majesties Subjects*, to *Trade* into these parts.

Its Air and Temperature.

This *Countrey* is blest with a sweet aud wholesome *Air*, and the *Clime* of late very agreeable to

the

Virginia now very healthful. the *English*, since the clearing of *Woods*; so that now few dyeth of the *Countreys* disease, called the *Seasoning*.

The Soyl.

It is every where interlaced with delectable *Hills*, and rich *Valleys*, and of a *Soyl* so Fertile, that an Acre of ground commonly yieldeth 200 *Bushels* of Corn, and is very apt to produce what is put therein, **The Soyl very Rich.** as *English Grains*, *Roots*, *Seeds*, *Plants*, *Fruits*, &c. besides those appropriated to the *Countrey*, and other adjacent parts of *America*.

Their Fruits.

Excellent Fruits. Here are excellent *Fruits* in great abundance, which may be compared with those of *Italy* or *Spain*, as *Apricocks*,

Virginia.

pricocks, *Peaches*, *Mellons*, *Apples*, *Pears*, *Plumbs*, *Cherries*, *Grapes*, *Figgs*, *Pomgranates*, *Quinces*, *Maracocks*, *Puchamines*, *Chesnuts*, *Walnuts*, *Olives*, *Strawberries*, *Rasberries*, *Goosberries*, and *Mulberries* in great abundance.

Of their *Apples* they make *Syder*; of their *Pears*, *Perry*; and of their *Grapes*, *Wine*.

Their Roots and Herbs.

They have several sorts of *Roots*, as *Potatoes*, *Carrets*, *Turnips*, *Artichoaks*, *Onyons*, *Cabbages*, *Collyflowers*, *Sparagus*, &c. And most sort of *Garden-herbs*, known to us in great plenty.

(marginal note: Plenty of Roots, & Herbs.)

Their Fowles, and Birds.

Abundance of Fowle. Here is great plenty of *Fowle*, as wild *Turkeys*, which usually weigh 6 stone; *Partridges, Swans, Geese, Ducks, Teal, Widgeons, Dotterels, Heathcocks, Oxeyes, Brants, Pidgeons, Cranes, Herons, Eagles*, and several sorts of *Hawkes*. And for small *Birds*, innumerable quantities of sundry sorts, as *Blackbirds, Thrushes, Redbirds*; and above all, the *Mockbird*, which counterfeiteth the notes of all Birds.

Their Wilde Beasts, and Tame Cattle.

They have great store of *wilde Beasts*, as *Lyons, Bears, Leopards, Tygers, Wolves*, and Dogs like *Wolves*

Virginia.

Wolves, but barke not; *Buffeloes, Elks*, whose Flesh is as good as Beef; *Rosconnes, Utchunquois, Deer, Hares, Bevers, Ottors, Foxes, Martins, Poulcats, Wesells, Musk-Rats, Flying Squirils*, &c. And for *Tame Cattle, Cowes, Sheep, Goats, Hoggs*, and *Horses* in great plenty.

Virginia well stored with Beasts, & Tame Cattle.

Their Fish.

Here is great plenty of Excellent *Fish*, as well in the *Sea*, and Bay of *Chesopeack*, as in the *Rivers*, viz. *Cods, Thornback, Sturgeon, Grampuses, Porpuses, Drums, Cat-Fish, Basses, Sheepsheads* (which makes broath like that of *Mutton*) *Cony-Fish, Rock-Fish, Creey-Fish, White Salmons, Mullets, Soles, Plaice, Mackrel, Trouts, Perches, Conger-Eels, Herrings, Crabs, Oysters, Shrimps, Cockles, Muscles,* &c.

Variety of Fish.

Commodities.

The Product of the Country

Commodities which this Countrey doth, or may produce, are *Hemp, Flax, Hops, Rape-Seed, Annicefeed, Woad, Madder, Pot-Ashes, Honey, Wax, Silk,* (if they would make it, *Mulberry-Trees* here growing in such great plenty) *Saxafras, Sarsaparilla,* several sweet *Gums,* and *Balsomes* of Sovereign vertues, several sorts of *Plants, Woods,* &c. used by *Dyers,* here are veins of *Alomes, Iron,* and *Copper,* sundry sorts of Rich *Furrs, Elk-skins* (which maketh excellent *Buffe*) and other *Hides*; *Pitch, Tarr, Rozen, Turpentine, Butter, Cheese,* and *Salted Flesh* and *Fish,* which find vent at the *Barbadoes,* and other *Caribbe Isles*; but above all these, their chief *Commodity* is *Tobacco,*

bacco, which they are sure to find vent for, and is the Standard by which all other *Commodities* are prized; but it were well for the *Inhabitants* if they would imploy their time, about the making of *Silk*, or some other *Commodities*, which in a short time would be found more advantageous, unto them, & then their *Tobacco* would not be so great a Drug as of late it is, insomuch that the *Merchant* ofttimes had rather lose it, then to pay the charges and Duties of *Freight, Custome, Excise*, &c.

Here groweth a kind of *Flax*, called *Silk-grass*, of which the *Indians* make *Thred*, and *Strings*, and is good to make *Linnen-cloth*, and *Shifts*, and would make excellent strong *Cables*.

Virginia.

Their Trade.

Here all *Trades-men*, especially *Handicrafts* finds good encouragement; and for those *Commodities* aforesaid, the *English* (who have the sole *Trade*) bring them all sorts of *Apparel*, all manner of *Utinsills*, belonging to *Houshold-stuf*, or necessary in their *Plantations*, or otherwise; also *Wine*, *Brandy*, and other strong *Drinks*; likewise all *Silks*, *Stuf* and *Cloth*, both *Linnen* and *Wollen*, which they convert to several uses according to their Fancyes, being now supplyed by *Taylors*.

Their Trees.

Here groweth sundry sorts of *Trees*, of the red and white *Oak*, *Black*

Virginia.

Black Walnut, Cedar, Pine, Cyprus, Chesnut, Poppler, Ash, Elm, &c. many of which are very good for the building of *Ships*, and other uses.

Several good Woods.

The Rivers.

This Country is well watered with several great, and strong *Rivers* which lose themselves in the Gulph or bay of Chesopeak, which gives entrance for shipping in this *Country*, as also to *Mary-Land* next adjoyning; which said *Bay* is very large, Capacious, and Comodious for *Shipping*, being said to run up into the *Countrey* northwards near 75 Leagues; its breadth in many places, being 5, 6, or 7 Leagues, and sometimes more, and 6 or 7 Fathom deep, and its opening to the South between *Cape-Henry*

Henry, which begineth *Virginia*, and *Cape-Charles* on the other side opposite, being about 10, or 12 *Leagues* wide.

Its chief Rivers. The principal of these *Rivers* begining at *Cape-Henry*, are *Pawhatan*, now called *James-River*, being very large & Commodious for ships, and found navigable about 50 *Leagues*. *Pamaunke*, now *York-River*, also large and *Navigable*, about 20 Leagues. *Rapahanock* or *Toppahanock*, likewise a good River and *Navigable*, about 40. Leagues, which is the last River of *Virginia* Northwardly, that falls into the *Bay* of *Chesopeack*.

Their Townes.

Upon, or near, these *Rivers* for the conveniency of shipping, the

Virginia.

the *English* are seated, which at present do amount unto the number of about 30, or 40000, and have some *Townes*, the chief amongst which, is *James-Town*, or rather *James City*, commodiously seated on *James-River*; the *Town* is beautified with many fair and well built Brick Houses, and as it is the chief town of the *Countrey*; here is kept the *Courts* of *Judicature* and *Offices* of publique concern; not far from which, at *Green-Spring*, resideth the *Governour* Sir *William Berkley*. *James Town.*

Next to *James-town* may be reckoned that of *Elizabeth*, seated at the mouth of the said River, a well built Town. *Elizabeth Town.*

Also *Dales-gift*, *Wicocomoco*, *Bermuda*, and others. *Dales Gift.*

Virginia.

The English Government.

Virginia under a good Government.
This *Countrey* is Governed by *Laws* agreeable with those of *England*, for the deciding of all *Causes* both *Civil* and *Criminal*; which said *Laws* are thus made by the *Governour*, appointed by his *Majesty*, with the consent of the *General Assembly*, which doth consist of his *Council*, and the *Burgesses* chosen by the *Free-holders*.

And for the better *Government*, the *Countrey*, which is possessed by the *English*, is divided into several *Counties*, in each of which are *Sheriffs*, *Justices* of the *Peace*, and other *Officers*, which are from time to time appoynted by the *Governour*; The names of the *Counties* are those of *Carotuck*, *Charles*, *Glocester*, *Hartford*, *Henrico*,

The Counties

Virginia.

rico, *James*, *New-Kent*, *Lancaſtar*, *Middleſex*, *Nanſemund*, *Lower-Norfolk*, *Northampton*, *Northumberland*, *Rappahanock*, *Surrey*, *Warwick*, *Weſtmorland*, *Iſle of Wight*, and *York*, and in each of theſe *Counties*, are held petty *Courts*, every month from which there may be *Appeales* to the *Quarter-Court* held at *James-Town*.

The Natives or Indians.

Virginia was, and yet is the habitation of divers ſorts of *Indians*, which have no dependance upon each other, being of particular *Tribes*, and having their peculiar King to Govern them; every *Indian-Town*, or rather poor *Village*, being the habitation of a *King*; and theſe *People* do rather live

live at enmity, than amity together. And as to their *Dispositions*, *Manners*, *Religions*, &c. there is found a difference, but most of all in their *Languages*; so that those *People* may not improperly be called so many several *Nations*.

They are generally a sort of people well proportionate, stout, of a swarthy complexion, their Hair black, and flaggy, which they wear long; they are of a ready Wit, very Subtile, and Treacherous, not much addicted to labour, being too great lovers of their ease; they are much given to *Hunting*, and going to *Wars* with each other, their Weapons being the *Bow* and *Arrows*, at which they are very expert, being good marks-men; but of late they have got the use of *Guns*, and other *Weapons*, through the folly of the English in shewing

Virginia.

shewing them. They are very loving and obedient to their *Kings*; in *matters* of *Religion*, they observe strange *Ceremonies*, and their *Priests* (which are esteemed *Conjurers*) makes *Sacrifices* for them. They believe the *Transmigration* of the *Soul*, and have strange fancies about the *Creation* of they *World*, they believe there is a God, but think he hath something else to do then to concern himself with things below, as too inferiour for him, and do therefore not Worship him; but the *Divel* they worship out of a fear, least he should destroy them, as having the power of them.

Their *Apparel* is but mean, only contenting themselves with something to cover their Nakedness; and for the better defending themselves from the weather, they

_{Their Apparel}

they anoynt their Bodyes with certain *Oyles* mixt with *Beares Greafe.*

<small>Their Houfes.</small> Their *Houfes* are no better then our *Englifh Hogfties,* and are made of *Boughs,* and covered with *Bark* of *Trees* ; and in the midft thereof, is placed their *Chimney,* or *Fire-place.*

<small>Their Dyet.</small> Their *Dyet* in meanefs, is anfwerable to their Houfes, not endeavouring to pleafe their *Pallets* with curious *Sauces,* or pompering their Bodies with provokative *Meates.*

A DESCRIPTION OF MARYLAND.

Its Scituation and Bounds.

THE *Province* of *Maryland* lying between the degrees of 37, and 50 *minutes*, or thereabouts, and 40 degrees of *Northern Latitude*. It hath for its Bounds on the South, *Virginia*, (from which it is parted by the River *Patowmeck*,

meck, whose Southerly bank divides the Province from *Virginia*;) on the *East,* the *Atlantick Ocean,* and *Delaware-Bay*; on the North, *New-England,* and *New-York,* formerly part of *New-England,* lying on the East side of *Delaware-Bay*; and on the West, the true *Meridian* of the first fountain of the River of *Patowmeck.*

Chesopeak Bay. The *Bay* of *Chesopeack* giving entrance to *Ships* into *Virginia,* and *Maryland,* passeth through the heart of this *Province,* and is found Navigable near 200 *miles*; into which falls the Rivers of *Patowmeck, Patuxent, Ann-Arundel,* (alas *Severn*) and *Sasquesahanough,* lying on the West side of the *Bay*; and to the East of the said *Bay,* those of *Choptanke, Nantecoke, Pocomoke,* and several other *Rivers* and *Rivulets,* to the great improve-

Its Rivers.

Maryland.

improvement of the Soyl, and Beauty of this *Province*.

The Countrey of late, since the Felling of the *Woods*, and the *Peoples* accustoming themselves to *English Dyet*, is very healthful and and agreeable to the constitution of the *English*, few now dying at their first coming, of the *Countreys disease*, or *Seasoning*. And as to the Temperature of *Air*, the *heats* in *Summer*, receive such seasonable allayes from gentle breezes, and fresh Showres of Rain; and the *Cold* in *Winter*, is of so little durance, that the *Inhabitants* cannot be said to suffer by either.

The Country *very healthful*

The Soyl, &c.

The *Countrey* is generally plain and even, yet rising in some places into small and pleasant Hills, which

which heighten the beauty of the adjacent *Valleys*.

The *Soyl* is Rich and Fertil, naturally producing all such *Commodities* as are in the precedent discourse set down as peculiar to its neighbouring Colony, *Virginia*; as all sorts of *Beasts* and *Fowle* both Tame and Wild, *Fish*, *Fruits*, *Plants*, *Roots*, *Herbs*, *Gums*, *Trees*, *Balsomes*, &c. as likewise all *Commodities* produced by Industry, are here found in as great plenty and perfection: But the general trade of *Maryland* depends chiefly upon *Tobacco*, which being esteemed better for a Forreign *Market* than that of *Virginia*, finds great Vent abroad, and the *Planters* at home; in exchange thereof, are furnished by the *Merchant* with all necessaries, for himself, his *House*, *Family*, and *Plantation*.

For the Beasts, Fowl, Fish, Fruits, &c. See in the Description of Virginia.

There

Maryland.

Their Coyns, & way of Trade.

Their is a Competent stock of ready mony in this *Province* both of *English*, Forreign, and his Lordshipps own *Coyne*, yet their chief way of *Commerce* is by way of barter, or exchange of *Commodities*, which may be judged to be no wayes inconsiderable, since 100 sail of *Ships* from *England*, and the English *Plantations*, have of late Yeares been known to trade thither in one Year.

The Natives.

The *Natives*, as to their *Complexion*, *Stature*, *Customes*, *Dispositions*, *Laws*, *Religions*, *Apparel*, *Dyet*, *Houses*, &c. are much the same as those of *Virginia*, already treated of; being likewise many different *Tribes*, or sorts of People, and each Govern'd by their particular *King*.

Maryland.

The Government, &c. of this Countrey.

This *Province* of *Maryland*, his *Majesty* King *Charles* the first in *Anno* 1632, granted by *Patent* to the Right Honourable *Cæcilius Calvert*, Lord *Baltemore*, and to his *Heires* and Assignes; and by that Patent created him, and them, the true and absolute *Lords* and *Propriators* of the same, (saving the Allegiance and Soveraigne Dominion due to his *Majesty*, his *Heirs*, and *Successours*;) thereby likewise granting to them all *Royal Jurisdictions*, and *Prerogatives* both *Military* and *Civil*; as power of enacting *Laws*, *Martial Laws*, making of *War*, and *Peace*, pardoning of *Offences*, Conferring of *Honours*, *Coyning of*

Maryland well Governed.

Maryland.

of *Money*, &c. And in acknowledgement thereof, yeilding and and paying yearly to his Majesty, his *Heires* and Successors, two *Indian Arrows* at *Windsor Castle* in the County of *Berks*, on *Easter Tuesday*; together with the fifth part of all the *Gold* and *Silver Oare* that shall be found there.

For the better inviting of people to settle here, his Lordship, by advice of the General *Assembly* of that *Province*, hath long since established a *Model* of good and wholsome *Laws* for the ease and benefit of the *Inhabitants*, with tolleration of *Religion*, to all sorts that profess the Faith of *Christ*: which hath been a principal motive to many to settle under that *Government*, rather then in another where liberty of Conscience was denyed them.

Maryland.

Its division into Countyes.

The Names of the Counties

This *Province* where it is peopled with *English*, is severed into 10 *Counties*; to wit, 5 Eastwards of *Chesopeak* Bay, as *Cecil, Dorchester, Kent, Sommerset,* and *Talbot*; and 5 westwards of the said Bay, as *Ann-Arundel, Baltemore, Calvert, Charles,* and St. *Maries*. And in every one of these *Countyes*, there is held an inferiour *Court* every two months for small matters, from which there lyeth Appeales to the *Provincial Court*, held at St. *Maryes*. Here are likewise certain *Magistrates* appoynted by his Lordship in each *County*, as *Sheriffs, Justices* of the *Peace*, &c.

Their

Maryland.

Their Townes.

The Inhabitants (being in number at present about 16000) have begun the building of several *Townes*, which in few Yeares 'tis hoped may come to some perfection; as *Calverton, Herrington,* and *Harvy-Town,* all Commodiously seated for the benefit of *Trade,* and conveniency of *Shipping,* but the principal Town is *St. Maryes,* seated on *St. Georges River,* being beautified with divers well-built *Houses,* and is the cheif place or scale of *Trade* for the *Province,* where the *Governour* his Lordships Son and Heir, Mr. *Charles Calvert* hath his *House,* and where the *General Assembly,* and *Provincial Courts* are held, and *Publique Offices* kept;

S. *Maries* Town.

kept; but at present the said *Governour* doth reside at *Mattapany*, about 8 Miles distant where he hath a fair and pleasant *House*. And for the better assisting the said *Governour*, in matters that concerns the *Government* of the *Province*, he hath his Council, &c.

A

A DESCRIPTION OF New-YORK.

Adjoyning to *Mary-Land*, Northwards, is a Colony called *New-York*, from his *Royal Highness* the Duke of *York*, the *Proprietor* thereof by grant from his Majesty, and is that part of *New-England* which the *Dutch* formerly seized, and called the New-Netherlands.

Its Fertility, &c.

This Country very Fertile.

It is a *Countrey*, of a Rich and Fertile *Soyl*, well watered with *Rivers*, as is *Mary-Land* already spoken of, and is found to produce the same *Beasts, Birds, Fish, Fruits, Commodities, Trees,* &c. and in as great plenty.

Its Town.

New York

Here is one very considerable *Town*, first built by the *Dutch*, and called *New-Amsterdam*, which name is now changed to *New-York*: It is well seated both for *Trade, Security*, and *Pleasure*, in a small *Isle* called *Mahatan*, reguarding the *Sea*, made so by *Hudsons-River*, which severeth it from *Long-Island*, which said River is very com-

commodious for *Shipping*, and is about two *Leagues* broad. The *Town* is large, containing about five hundred well-built *Houses*; and for Civil *Government*, it hath a *Mayor*, *Alderman*, a *Sheriff*, and *Justices* of the *Peace* for their *Magistrates*. For the further security of this *Town*, here is raised a *Fort* called *James-Fort*, which is very strong, and well Defended and Maintained with *Men*, and *Ammunition*. The *Town* is Inhabited by the *English*, and *Dutch*, and hath a considerable *Trade* with the *Indians*, for the *Skins* of *Elks*, *Deer*, *Bears*, &c. also for those of *Bever*, *Otter*, and other *Furrs*; and doth likewise enjoy a good *Trade* with the *English*.

The Natives,

This Countrey is also possessed with sundry sorts of people, not much unlike the *Indians* of *Virginia*, being well-*proportioned*, *Stout*, *Swarthy*, *Black haired*, very expert in their *Bow*, and *Arrows*, which are their chief weapons of War. They are courteous to the *English*, of a ready Witt, and very apt to receive Instructions from them; upon the least Offence, the man turneth away his wife, and marrieth again, and the *Children* begotten by her, she taketh with her, the *man* not regarding them. *Fornication* is here permitted. They observe several *Ceremonies* in their *Religious Rites*, and are said to worship the *Devil*, whom they greatly fear. Their *Priests* are no

The Disposition of the Natives.

New-York.

no better than *Sorcerers*, who strangly bewitch these silly *Creatures*. When any woman findeth her self quick with *Child*, she keepeth her self chast, or untouched by man until her delivery, the like she observeth in the time of her giving Suck. A strange custom which our *European Dames* would not well like of! They are very obedient and loving to their *Kings*: They believe the *Transmigration* of the *Soul*; and concerning the Creation of the *World*, have a strange fantastical opinions. They are much addicted to *Dancing*, *Sports*, and *Recreations*, observing *Festival Times*.

Their *Habit* is but mean, as the rest of the *Indians*, yet do they *Paint* and besmear their *Faces* with several *Colours* by way of Ornament.

Their Habit & Dyet, &c.

Their

There *Dyet* and *Habitations* are also as mean.

They are much addicted to go to *Wars* against one another, and do seldome give quarter to any, but the *Women* and *Children*, whom they preserve, and make use of for the encreasing their strength.

A DESCRIPTION OF New-ENGLAND.

Its Situation.

NEw *England* is seated North of *Maryland*, which according to the report of Capt. *Smith*, hath 70 miles of *Sea Coast*, where are found divers good *Havens*, some of which are capable to harbour 500 *Saile* of *Shipps* from the fury the of *Sea*, and *Winds*, by reason of the in-

interposition of several *Isles* (to the number of about 200) which lie about this *Coast*.

Its Scituation. And although this *Countrey* is seated in the midst of the *Temperate Zone*, yet is the *Clime* more uncertain, as to *Heat* and *Cold*, then those *European Kingdomes*, which lie *Parallel* with it; and as to *Virginia*, this may be compared as *Scotland* is to *England*.

The Aire.

The Ayr. The *Aire* is here found very healthful, and very agreeable to the *English*, which makes them possess many potent *Colonyes*.

Its Inhabitants.

This *Countrey* is possessed by di-

divers sorts of *People*, who are *Governed* by their particular *Kings*, and do much differ in *Customes*, and *Manners*, from one another, as those *Indians* inhabiting in *Maryland*, *Virginia*, and other parts of *America*. And do live generally at variance with each other. They have their several *Townes* and *settlements*, and their Riches doth consist in their *Furs*, and *Skins*, which they sell to the *English*.

The Disposition of the Natives much like those of Virginia.

When first inhabited by the English.

This *Countrey* became first to be a *Colony* of the *English* about the *Year* 1605, being granted by *Patent* from *King James*, to certain proprietors under the name of the *Plymouth Company*; but divers years were spun out, with great
ex-

expences, and not without sundry casualties befalling on the *Adventurers*, before it became any thing considerable, and in a setled condition.

Their Rivers, and Fish.

This *Country* is well watered with *Rivers*, the chief amongst which, are *Agamentico, Conectecut, Kinebequy, Merrimeck, Mishuin, Mistick, Neraganset, Pascataway, Pemnaquid, Tachobacco,* &c. and in these *Rivers*, together with the Sea, are taken excellent *Fish*, as *Cod, Thornback, Sturgeon, Porpuses, Haddock, Salmons, Herrings, Mackeril, Oysters, Lobsters, Crab-Fish, Tortoise, Cocles, Muscles, Clams, Smelts, Eels, Lamprons, Alewives, Basses, Hollibuts, Sharks, Seales, Grampus,* and *Whales.*

Excellent Fish.

Their

Their Fowles, and Birds.

Here are great variety of Fowls, as *Phesants, Partridges, Heath-Cocks, Turkeys, Geess, Ducks, Hernes, Cranes, Cormorants, Swans, Widgins, Sheldrakes, Snipes, Doppers, Blackbirds,* the *Humbird, Loon,* &c.

Their Beasts, both Tame and Wild.

Their *Wild Beasts* of chief note, are *Lyons, Beares, Foxes, Rackoons, Mooses, Musquashs, Otters, Bevers, Deer, Hares, Coneys,* &c. and for *Tame Beasts, Cowes, Sheep, Goates, Swine,* and *Horses.*

Amongst the hurtful *things* in this *Countrey,* the *Rattle-Snake* is most dangerous. Here are also several

Hurtfull things.

several sorts of Stinging *Flyes*, which are found very troublesome to the *Inhabitants*.

Their Trees, and Fruits.

Fruits.

Here are sundry sorts of *Trees*, as the *Oak*, *Cyprus*, *Pine*, *Chesnut*, *Cedar*, *Walnut*, *Firr*, *Ash*, *Asp*, *Elm*, *Alder*, *Maple*, *Birch*, *Sasafras*, *Sumach*, several *Fruit-Trees*, as *Apples*, *Pears*, *Plumbs*, with several others that are growing in *Virginia*, and *Mary-land*, which I have already took notice of.

Their Commodities, and Trade.

Commodities & Trade.

This *Countrey* affordeth several sorts of rich *Furrs*, *Flax*, *Linnen*, *Amber*, *Iron*, *Pitch*, *Tarr*, *Cables*, *Masts*, and *Timber* to build *Ships*, also several sorts of *Grain*, &c.

The

New England.

The Inhabitants drive a considerable Trade to *Barbadoes*, and other our *American Plantations*, in supplying them with *Flower, Bisket, Salt, Flesh*, and *Fish*, &c. and in return bring *Sugars*, and other *Commodities*, as well for their own use, as to sell again. They also drive a considerable Trade with *England* for *wearing Apparrel, Stuffs, Silks, Cloth*, several *Utensils* for their *Houses, Iron, Brass*, and such like things that are useful to man and not found amongst them.

As to the *Coyns, Weights*, and *Measures* of *New-England*, and the rest of the *American Plantations* belonging to his *Majesty*, they are the same with those of *London*, but as to *Coyns*, they are not much made use of in *Trade*, their way being bartering of one *Commodi-*

ty for another; but at *Jamaica* they have plenty of *Spanish Coins,* and at *Barbadoes* those of *England.*

The *English* now Inhabiting in *New-England,* are very numerous, and powerful, having a great many Towns, many of which are considerable.

The *English* Government.

The Government of the Inhabitants of New-England.

The *Inhabitants* are *Governed* by *Laws* of their own making, and have their several *Courts,* and places of *Judicature,* and assemble together, at their set times, and places, as well for the making of New *Lawes,* abolishing of Old, Hearing, and Determining of *Causes;* as for the Election of a *Governour, Deputy-Governour, Assistants, Burgesses,* and other *Magistrates,* (every Town having two *Burgesses*) each *County* Annually

ally Electing such like *Officers*, for the looking after the like *Affairs* in the said *Colony*. And in matters that concern *Religion*, and *Church-Government*, they are very strict and make a great shew, being much of the stamp of the Ridgid *Presbyterians*.

The Towns.

Here are several Towns, as *Boston*, the *Metropolis* of *New-England*, Commodiously seated for *Traffique* on the *Sea-Shore*; It is at present a very large and spacious *Town*, or rather *City*, composed of several well-ordered *Streets*, and graced with fair and beautiful *Houses*, which are well Inhabited by *Merchants*, and *Tradesmen*, who drive a considerable *Trade* for such *Commodities* as the *Countrey* affordeth,

Boston.

eth to *Barbadoes*, and the other *Caribbee Isles*, as also to *England*, and *Ireland*; taking in exchange such *Commodities* as each place affordeth, or are found useful to them. It is a place of a good strength, having two or three *Hills* adjoyning, on which are raised *Fortifications*, with great *Peices* mounted thereon, which are well guarded.

Charles Town.   *Charles-Town*, seated on and between the Rivers *Charles* and *Mistick*; it is beautified with a large and well-built *Church*, and near the River side is the *Market-place*, from which runneth two *Streets*, in which are divers good *Houses*.

Dorchester.   *Dorchester* scituate near the *Sea*, where there falleth in two *Rivulets*. An indifferent *Town*.

Cambridg   *Cambridg*, formerly *New-Town* seated on the River *Merrimeck*: this Town consisteth of several *Streets*

New-England.

Streets, and is beautified with two *Colledges*, and divers fair, and well built *Houses*.

St. Georges-Fort, seated on the mouth of the River *Sagadebock*. St. Georges Fort.

New-Plimouth, seated on that large *Bay* of *Potuxed*.

Reading, commodiously seated about a great *Pond*, and well-watered, and *Inhabited*. In this Town are two *Mills*, one for *Corn*, and the other for *Timber*. Reading.

Salem, pleasantly seated betwixt two *Rivers*. Salem.

Other Towns placed Alphabetically.

Berwick, Braintree, Bristol, Concord, Dartmouth, Dedham, Dover, Exeter, Falmouth, Glocester, Greens-Harbour, Hampton, Hartford, Haverhil, Hingham, Hull, Ipswich, Lin,

Lin, Maulden, New-bury, New-Havon, Northam, Norwich, Oxford, Rowley, Roxbury, Salisbury, Sandwich, Southampton, Spring-field, Sudbury, Taunton, Water-Town, Wenham, Weymouth, Woburne, and *Yarmouth.*

Most of these *Towns* beareth the names from those in *England,* and many of them are of good account, being commodiously seated, either on the Sea-Shore, or on Navigable *Rivers,* and are well Inhabited. And most of those *Towns* are known to the *Indians* by other Names.

A DESCRIPTION OF NEW-FOUND-LAND.

NEwfoundland is an *Island* in Extent equal to *England*, from whence it is distant little above 600 *Leagues*, lying near half way between *Ireland*, and *Virginia*.

Its Scituation.

It is *scituated* betwixt the degrees of 46, and 53 of Northern *Latitudes*, and it is only severed from the Continent of *America*, by an Arm of the *Sea,* like that which separates *England* from *France.*

Its Bays, Rivers, Fish, Fowl, Beasts, &c.

Its Bayes and Rivers.   It is Famous for many spacious and excellent *Bayes,* and *Harbours,* and within the *Land* for the variety of Fresh *Springs,* whose waters are exceeding delicious.

Its Fish, Fowles, Beasts,   It is enriched by nature, with plenty of *Fish, Land,* and *Water-Fowl,* and sufficiently stockt with *Deer, Hares, Otters, Foxes, Squirils,* and other *Beasts* which yield good *Furrs:* And though not over-run generally with *Woods,* it doth afford (besides store of *Fewel*) abundance of stately *Trees,* fit for *Timber, Masts, Planks,* and sundry other uses.

Trees.

The

The ſoile and Climate.

The *Soile* in moſt places is reputed fertile; the Climate wholſome, though the rigour of the *winter* ſeaſon, and the exceſs of *Heats* in *Summer*, doth detract ſomething from its due praiſe.

How Inhabited.

The North and Weſt part of this *Countrey* the *Native-Indians* Inhabit, though but few in number, and thoſe a more rude and ſavage ſort of People then thoſe of *New-England* and other places in the adjacent Contenent, already taken notice of.

Its Inhabitants.

New-found-Land first discovered by the English.

The English the true Proprietors of New-Foundland

The *Island*, of *New-found Land* was first discovered by the *English*, who are the true *Propriators* thereof, excluding all Forreigne right, and justifying the same to belong to the Crown of *England* only, whose Interest hath been there continued by several, under the Reigns of divers *Kings* & *Queens*.

The Ld. Baltemore the proprietor of Avalon in New-Foundland.

In the year 1623, Sir *George Calvert* Knight, then *Principal Secretary* of *State*, and afterwards L^d. *Baltemore*, obtained a *Patent* of part of *New-found-land*; which was erected into a *Province*, and called *Avalon*; where he caused a Plantation to be setled, and a stately *House* and *Fort* to be built at *Ferryland*, and afterwards Transported himself

self and Family thither, and continuing the *Plantation* by his *Deputy*, till by descent (after his Lordships decease) it came to his son and heir the Right Honorable *Cæcilius*, now Lord *Baltemore*, who by *Deputies* from time to time, was no less careful to preserve his Interest there, which (though during the late troubles in *England*, it was by Sir *David Kirkes* means, for some years discontinued, he was soon re-invested in the same by his Majesties most happy Restauration.

There is no part of *New-found-land* generally more happy for multiplicity of excellent *Bayes*, and *Harbours*, then this *Province*, and where vast quantities of *Fish* are yearly caught by the *English*; especially at *Ferryland*, and the *Bay* of *Bulls*. But the whole *Coast* of the *Island*, affords infinite plenty of

Codd,

Codd, and *Poor-John,* which is the chief *Commodity* of the *Isle,* which is grown to a setled *Trade,* for these many years, to the *enrichment* of all those that Trade thither.

A great bank of Land.

<small>A great bank of Land.</small>

East of *Newfoundland,* over against *Cape-Ray,* at the distance of about 70 *miles,* lyeth a great Bank of Land, of about 300 *miles* in Length, and not above Seventy-five in Breadth, where broadest. It lyes under the *Sea* many *Fathoms* deep, so the *Ships* of a considerable Burthen may ride over it: and about this Banck lyes dispersed several small *Isles,* called by St. *Sebastion Cabot* (the first discoverer) *Los Baccaloos,* or the Isles of *Cod-fish,* from the prodigious quantities of *Cod-Fish* there found

found, which were said to obstruct the passage of his *Vessels*.

The Trade to this Island.

The *French*, *Dutch*, *Biscaners*, and other *Nations* that yearely *Trade* hither amounting to between 3 or 400 *Vessels*, are assured to find sufficient *Freight* of *Cod* and *Poor John*, which they find good vent for in the *Streights*, *Spaine*, *France*, and other *Countreys* to their great profit and encouragement.

A great Trade here driven.

And were the *English* diligent to inspect the advantage that might accrue to this *Nation*, by settling *Plantations* on the Island, and raising *Fortifications*, for the security of the place; we might give Law to all forreigners that come to *Fish* there, and in few years

Years engross the whole *Fishery* to our selves: the greatest *Ballance* perchance of *Forraigne Trade*.

FINIS.

www.ingramcontent.com/pod-product-compliance
Lightning Source LLC
Chambersburg PA
CBHW020913230426
43666CB00008B/1439